CliffsNotes™

The Adventures of Tom Sawyer

By James L. Roberts, Ph.D.

IN THIS BOOK

- Learn about the Life and Background of the Author
- Preview an Introduction to the Novel
- Study a graphical Character Map
- Explore themes and literary devices in the Critical Commentaries
- Examine in-depth Character Analyses
- Enhance your understanding of the work with Critical Essays
- Reinforce what you learn with CliffsNotes Review
- Find additional information to further your study in CliffsNotes Resource Center and online at www.cliffsnotes.com

Wiley Publishing, Inc.

About the Author

A Fulbright scholar at the University of Vienna, James L. Roberts is Professor Emeritus at the University of Nebraska-Lincoln. He has taught extensively at major universities throughout the world.

Publisher's Acknowledgments

Editorial

Project Editor: Tracy Barr

Acquisitions Editor: Greg Tubach

Glossary Editors: The editors and staff at Webster's New World Dictionaries

Editorial Administrator: Michelle Hacker

Production

Indexer: York Production Services, Inc.

Proofreader: York Production Services, Inc.

Wiley Indianapolis Composition Services

CliffsNotes™ *The Adventures of Tom Sawyer*
Published by:
Wiley Publishing, Inc.
909 Third Avenue
New York, NY 10022
www.wiley.com

Table of Contents

How to Use This Book

This CliffsNotes study guide on Mark Twain's *The Adventures of Tom Sawyer* supplements the original literary work, giving you background information about the author, an introduction to the work, a graphical character map, critical commentaries, expanded glossaries, and a comprehensive index, all for you to use as an educational tool that will allow you to better understand *The Adventures of Tom Sawyer.* This study guide was written with the assumption that you have read *The Adventures of Tom Sawyer.* Reading a literary work doesn't mean that you immediately grasp the major themes and devices used by the author; this study guide will help supplement your reading to be sure you get all you can from Mark Twain's *The Adventures of Tom Sawyer.* CliffsNotes Review tests your comprehension of the original text and reinforces learning with questions and answers, practice projects, and more. For further information on Mark Twain and *The Adventures of Tom Sawyer*, check out the CliffsNotes Resource Center..

CliffsNotes provides the following icons to highlight essential elements of particular interest:

Reveals the underlying themes in the work.

Helps you more easily relate to or discover the depth of a character.

Uncovers elements such as setting, atmosphere, mystery, passion, violence, irony, symbolism, tragedy, foreshadowing, and satire.

Enables you to appreciate the nuances of words and phrases.

Don't Miss Our Web Site

Discover classic literature as well as modern-day treasures by visiting the CliffsNotes Web site at www.cliffsnotes.com. You can obtain a quick download of a CliffsNotes title, purchase a title in print form, browse our catalog, or view online samples.

LIFE AND BACKGROUND OF THE AUTHOR

The following abbreviated biography of Mark Twain is provided so that you might become more familiar with his life and the historical times that possibly influenced his writing. Read this Life and Background of the Author section and recall it when reading Twain's *The Adventures of Tom Sawyer*, thinking of any thematic relationship between Twain's novel and his life.

Personal Background

Mark Twain (a.k.a., Samuel Langhorne Clemens) was born in the little town of Florida, Missouri, on November 30, 1835, shortly after his family had moved there from Tennessee. When Twain was about four, his family moved again, this time to Hannibal, Missouri, a small town of about five hundred people.

Twain's father was a lawyer by profession but was only mildly successful. He was, however, highly intelligent and a stern disciplinarian. Twain's mother, a southern belle in her youth, had a natural sense of humor, was emotional, and was known to be particularly fond of animals and unfortunate human beings. Although the family was not wealthy, Twain apparently had a happy and secure childhood.

Early Career

Twain's father died when Twain was twelve years old and, for the next ten years, Twain was an apprentice printer and then a printer both in Hannibal and in New York City. Hoping to find his fortune, he conceived a wild scheme of making a fortune in South America. On a riverboat to New Orleans, he met a famous riverboat pilot who promised to teach him the trade for five hundred dollars. After completing his training, Twain piloted riverboats along the Mississippi for four years. During this time, he became familiar with the towns along the mighty River and became acquainted with the characters who would later inhabit many of his novels, especially *Tom Sawyer* and *Huck Finn*.

When the Civil War began, Twain's allegiance tended to be Southern due to his Southern heritage, and he briefly served in the Confederate militia. Twain's brother Orion convinced him to go west on an expedition, a trip which became the subject matter of a later work, *Roughing It*.

Writing Career

Even though some of his letters and accounts of traveling had been published, Twain actually launched his literary career with the short story "The Celebrated Jumping Frog of Calaveras County," published in 1865. This story brought him national attention, and Twain devoted the major portion of the rest of his life to literary endeavors. In addition to *The Adventures of Tom Sawyer*, some of Twain's most popular and widely read works include novels such as *The Prince and the Pauper* (1881),

Life on the Mississippi (1883), *A Connecticut Yankee in King Arthur's Court* (1889), and *Pudd'nhead Wilson* (1894), as well as collections of short stories and essays, such as *The 1,000,000 Bank-Note and Other Stories* (1893), *The Man That Corrupted Hadleyburg and Other Essays* (1900), and *What Is Man?* (1906).

Mark Twain, one of America's first and foremost realists and humanists, was born in 1835 during the appearance of Haley's Comet, and he died during the next appearance of Haley's Comet, 75 years later.

INTRODUCTION TO THE NOVEL

The following Introduction section is provided solely as an educational tool and is not meant to replace the experience of your reading the novel. Read the Introduction and A Brief Synopsis to enhance your understanding of the novel and to prepare yourself for the critical thinking that should take place whenever you read any work of fiction or nonfiction. Keep the List of Characters and Character Map at hand so that as you read the original literary work, if you encounter a character about whom you're uncertain, you can refer to the List of Characters and Character Map to refresh your memory.

Introduction

The Adventures of Tom Sawyer, first published in 1875–76, is a child's adventure story; it is also, however, the story of a young boy's transition into a young man. In some ways, it is a *bildungsroman*, a novel whose principle subject is the moral, psychological, and intellectual development of a youthful main character. It is not a true *bildungsroman*, however, because Twain did not take Tom into full manhood.

One of America's best-loved tales, *Tom Sawyer* has a double appeal. First, it appeals to the young adolescent as the exciting adventures of a typical boy during the mid-nineteenth century, adventures that are still intriguing and delightful because they appeal to the basic instincts of nearly all young people, regardless of time or culture. Second, the novel appeals to the adult reader who looks back on his or her own childhood with fond reminiscences. In fact, in his preface to the first edition, Twain wrote, "Although my book is intended mainly for the entertainment of boys and girls . . . part of my plan has been to pleasantly remind adults of what they once were themselves, and what they felt and thought." Thus, the novel is a combination of the past and the present, of the well-remembered events from childhood told in such a way as to evoke remembrances in the adult mind.

Whether or not one has read the novel, many of the scenes are familiar and have become a part of our cultural heritage: Consider for example, the scene in which Tom manipulates others to paint a fence he himself was to have painted, the scene with Tom and Becky lost in the cave, and the scene of the boys in the graveyard. Twain captures the essence of childhood, with all its excitement, fear, and mischievousness. Likewise, the characters—Tom himself, Becky Thatcher, Huck Finn, Injun Joe, and Aunt Polly—have become part of our American heritage.

Although *Tom Sawyer* is set in a small town along the western frontier on the banks of the legendary Mississippi River sometime during the 1840s, readers from all parts of the world respond to the various adventures experienced by Tom and his band of friends. The appeal of the novel lies mostly in Twain's ability to capture—or re-capture—universal experiences and dreams and fears of childhood.

The Structure and Setting

In terms of the novel's structure, some critics have dismissed it as being simply a series of episodes. And it is true that there are many seemingly extraneous scenes; nevertheless, each scene contributes to building a broad picture of the lives of these youths. In the broadest sense, the novel concentrates basically on Tom's—and to a lesser degree, Huck's—development from carefree childish behavior to one that is filled with mature responsibility. Furthermore, the primary adventure—which features the murder the boys witness and its aftermath—provides a single event that begins in the graveyard and runs throughout the plot of lesser adventures. The lesser adventures are more episodic, which is typically Twain. *Adventures of Huckleberry Finn*, for example, is a series of episodes connected by the adventure to free the slave Jim.

Twain grew up in Hannibal, Missouri, a dusty, quiet town built on a bluff overlooking the Mississippi River about eighty miles north of St. Louis. This is the town—renamed St. Petersburg in the novel—that Tom and Huck and the other characters inhabit. The Jackson's Island of *Tom Sawyer* (which also appears in Twain's *Adventures of Huckleberry Finn*) is an actual island located just south of the town, close to the Illinois side of the river. The cave that Injun Joe inhabited still exists, as do the houses that the Widow Douglas and Aunt Polly supposedly inhabited. Twain's Hannibal was surrounded by large forests which Twain himself knew as a child and in which his characters Tom Sawyer and Joe Harper often play "Indians and Chiefs." The steamboats that passed daily were the fascination of the town, and Tom and Huck would watch their comings and goings from the bluff overlooking the Mississippi.

The Satire

Twain does not confine himself to telling a simple children's story. He is, as always, the satirist and commentator on the foibles of human nature. As the authorial commentator, Twain often steps in and comments on the absurdity of human nature. In *Tom Sawyer*, he is content with mild admonitions about the human race. For example, after Tom has tricked the other boys into painting the fence for him, the voice of Twain, the author, points out the gullibility of man: ". . . that in order to make a man or a boy covet a thing, it is only necessary to make the thing difficult to attain."

There are stronger satires. Twain is constantly satirizing the hypocrisy found in many religious observances. For example, in the Sunday school episode, there are aspects of religion satirized, as Twain points out that one boy had memorized so many verses of the Bible so as to win prizes—more Bibles elegantly illustrated—that "the strain upon his mental faculties was too great, and he was little better than an idiot from that day forward."

The adults' reaction to Injun Joe and his malevolence is a typical Twain commentary on society. The adults create petitions to free Joe who has already killed, so it was believed, five "citizens of the village, but what of that? If he had been Satan himself there would have been plenty of weaklings ready to scribble their names to a pardon petition, and drip a tear on it from their permanently impaired and leaky waterworks."

Twain criticizes the adult attitudes and behaviors throughout the novel. That is part of the conflict: the maturation of a youth (Tom) into adulthood conflicting with the disapproval of the adult behaviors that exist. It is this double vision that raises the novel above the level of a boy's adventure story.

Brief Synopsis

Aunt Polly searches and screams for Tom Sawyer: she wants to confront her nephew about some missing jam. Tom, however, is able to outwit his aunt and slips away. But Aunt Polly loves him so much she cannot be too harsh with him. She is concerned that he will play hooky that afternoon, and sure enough he does.

During the afternoon, Tom meets a boy from St. Louis with whom he fights. That night at home, Tom's clothes are so soiled from the fight that Aunt Polly punishes him by taking away his Saturday's freedom and assigns him the unpleasant task of whitewashing the fence.

On Saturday morning, the forlorn Tom begins his tedious task of whitewashing the fence, fully aware that all of his friends are playing in the town's square. As he begins his task, Aunt Polly's slave, Jim, comes by and Tom tries to bribe him into helping, but Aunt Polly sends Jim on his business. Suddenly, Tom is horrified because one of his friends is about to come by and see him actually working on a Saturday morning. Tom pretends that what he is doing is not work because he is so thoroughly enjoying himself. Soon Ben wants to try his hand and offers Tom his apple. As Ben is painting, other friends come by and also want to try their hands at this fun game. Each boy gives Tom some sort of prize for allowing him to do some whitewashing, and Tom ends up with his fence whitewashed and a small treasury of gifts.

After the fence is painted, Tom heads for the square and, on the way, stops to watch a very pretty young girl who is moving into a house down the street. He shows off for her, and she pretends to ignore him. He is attracted to her and finds out her name is Becky Thatcher. He joins his friends in fun and games where he is the leader of an army which defeats the opposing army. The next day, Sunday, he is forced to attend Sunday school and is bored with the tedium but finds ways to distract himself.

Monday, after offering many excuses for not going to school, he is finally forced to go. On the way, he meets Huckleberry Finn, the son of the town drunk. Huck never goes to school and is the envy of all the boys because of his complete freedom. Huck arranges for Tom to meet him that night so they can bury a dead cat in the cemetery. At school, Tom is punished for being late and is required to sit in the "girls' section." This pleases him because the only empty seat is next to Becky Thatcher. At lunch, he meets her, and they pledge their troth to each other.

At midnight, Huck arrives, and they go to the cemetery where they come upon Dr. Robinson, Injun Joe, and Muff Potter who are digging up a recently buried corpse. There is an argument, Muff is knocked unconscious, and Injun Joe murders the doctor and places the murder weapon next to Muff. The horrified boys flee and take a blood oath never to reveal what they have seen. The next day, the town is in an uproar (school is dismissed), and Injun Joe identifies Muff Potter as the murderer. Tom is fearful that Injun Joe will discover that he was a witness.

Tom, his friend Joe Harper, and Huck Finn decide to become pirates. The three boys find a raft and establish camp on Jackson's Island, where they enjoy a carefree life of fishing, swimming, smoking, and exploring and playing. When a steamboat filled with most of the important townspeople passes by firing cannons over the water, the boys realize that they are presumed to be drowned. Tom sneaks home at night in order to leave Aunt Polly a reassuring note that they are all right, but he changes his mind when he overhears that church services are planned for the "deceased boys" if they are not found by Sunday. The funeral services are secretly attended by the boys, and all rejoice when the dead boys casually stroll down the aisle.

Back at school, Tom finally wins Becky's heart when he takes the blame for one of her indiscretions and heroically suffers the punishment for her misdeeds.

At Muff Potter's trial, it is generally accepted that Muff Potter killed Dr. Robinson and will be hanged. Tom, in spite of his oath with Huck to not reveal what he has seen, cannot stand to see an innocent person hanged for a crime he did not commit. He bravely relates what actually happened. Injun Joe makes his escape by jumping out the second story window.

One day, while Tom and Huck are looking for buried treasure, they explore an old abandoned house. When two men arrive, the boys are trapped upstairs. One man is Injun Joe in disguise. The two criminals retrieve a box of silver coins they had concealed and then, by chance, discover a horde of gold coins that had been buried by some outlaws long ago. They decide to take the gold coins to Injun Joe's other hide out. The terrified boys overhear Injun Joe planning a horrible revenge before leaving the country. The boys fear that they are the subject of his planned vengeance but are fortunate enough to narrowly escape detection. The boys try to discover a place in town that would be the other hideout, but they only find a room filled with an abundant supply of whiskey in a Temperance Tavern.

At the picnic celebrating Becky Thatcher's birthday, several of the boys and girls enter McDougal's Cave. Tom and Becky wander away from the others in search of privacy and become hopelessly lost.

Meanwhile, Huck Finn, who is watching to discover Injun Joe's hideout, follows the two men toward Cardiff Hill, the home of the Widow Douglas and of a Welshman named Jones. Hiding behind a bush, he overhears Injun Joe telling of his intentions to mutilate the Widow Douglas because her husband, the judge, had once had him publicly horsewhipped. Huck hastens to inform Mr. Jones of the plot, and the Welshman and his sons drive off the vicious Injun Joe and his cohort. Huck has been so frightened that he becomes seriously ill, and the Widow Douglas comes to the Welshman's home and nurses the homeless boy back to health.

At the same time, it is discovered that Tom and Becky are missing; they have not been seen since the cave. All the available men in the community meet and carry out a thorough search of the cave. Tom and Becky hear the search party in the distance but are too weak to call loudly enough to be heard. At one point in their ordeal, Tom catches sight of Injun Joe in a nearby passage. After they have been underground for about three days, Tom discovers a way out of the cave. He and Becky then make their way back to the town.

Both are sick for a while, but Tom recovers more quickly than does Becky. Tom also discovers that Judge Thatcher has had the second exit to the cave completely sealed off. Tom reveals that Injun Joe was in the cave. In spite of Injun Joe's evil, Tom cannot let any human face the ordeal of starving that he and Becky just endured. The men go back to the cave and discover Injun Joe's body just inside the cave where he had futilely tried to dig his way out with a knife.

Later, Tom and Huck return to the cave and search for Injun Joe's treasure. After many false starts and using various clues, they recover approximately $12,000 worth of gold coins. This money is invested for them, and they are rich. The Widow Douglas takes Huck into her home to educate him and train him in the ways of civilization. Huck finds schooling, not cussing, and all other things connected with civilization to be completely intolerable, and he runs away. He eventually agrees to give civilized living another try if he can join Tom's band of robbers.

List of Characters

Tom Sawyer   The main character of the novel. Everything revolves around him, and, except for a few brief chapters, he is present in every chapter.

Aunt Polly   Tom's aunt and legal guardian. She loves Tom dearly, but she does not know how to control him.

Sidney   Tom's half brother who plays the role of the obedient boy but who is, in reality, a sneak and a tattletale.

Mary   Tom's cousin. She likes Tom very much but wants to change him and resorts to bribing him to be good.

Becky Thatcher   The pretty new girl to whom Tom is attracted. When trapped in the cave, she proves to be resolute and worthy of Tom's affections.

Huckleberry Finn (Huck)   The son of the town drunk, Huck has been the outcast from society his entire life. The adults look upon him as a disgrace and a bad influence; the youngsters look at him with envy because he has complete freedom to do whatever he likes.

Widow Douglas   The wealthiest person in the town, she is good, kindhearted, and generous. Because of her nature, Injun Joe's planned revenge—mutilating her—becomes that much more horrible. She is saved by the activities of Huck Finn and becomes his guardian.

Injun Joe   He is the villain, the essence of evil in the novel.

Muff Potter   The harmless old drunk who is framed for Dr. Robinson's murder (which was actually committed by Injun Joe).

Joe Harper   Tom's closest friend and second in command in Tom's adventures. He is not as clever as Tom is, nor is he the leader that Tom is. On Jackson's Island, Joe is the first to want to return to the security of home.

Judge Thatcher (and Mrs. Thatcher)   Becky's parents who are highly esteemed members of the community. The Judge uses his authority to seal up the opening to the cave to protect other youngsters and, in doing so, inadvertently seals up Injun Joe.

Mr. Dobbins   The schoolmaster. At the end of the school year, the entire school conspires to play a trick on him.

Mr. Walters   The Sunday school superintendent who is overly dedicated to his job.

The Reverend Mr. Sprague   The pastor of the village church.

Alfred Temple   A new boy from St. Louis. Becky uses him to make Tom jealous.

Willie Mufferson   The "model boy" for all of the parents and a despicable creature to all the boys.

Amy Lawrence   Tom's sweetheart—until he meets Becky Thatcher.

Dr. Robinson   The young doctor who is murdered while trying to obtain a body for medical studies.

Mr. Jones (or the Welshman)   He and his sons are instrumental in saving the Widow Douglas from the vicious Injun Joe.

Character Map

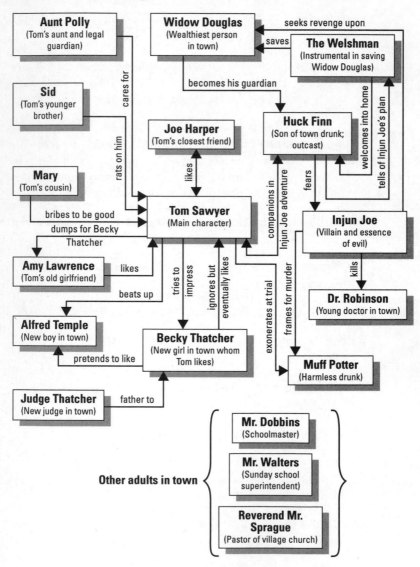

CRITICAL COMMENTARIES

The sections that follow provide great tools for supplementing your reading of *The Adventures of Tom Sawyer*. First, in order to enhance your understanding of and enjoyment from reading, we provide quick summaries in case you have difficulty when you read the original literary work. Each summary is followed by commentary: literary devices, character analyses, themes, and so on. Keep in mind that the interpretations here are solely those of the author of this study guide and are used to jumpstart your thinking about the work. No single interpretation of a complex work like *The Adventures of Tom Sawyer* is infallible or exhaustive, and you'll likely find that you interpret portions of the work differently from the author of this study guide. Read the original work and determine your own interpretations, referring to these Notes for supplemental meanings only.

Chapter I
Tom Plays, Fights, and Hides

Summary

Aunt Polly finds Tom in the pantry where he has been eating forbidden jam. As she gets a switch, Tom convinces her that something is behind her. As she turns, he escapes, leaving her to contemplate how he constantly plays tricks on her. She is concerned whether or not she is "doing her duty by him," but because he is her dead sister's child, she cannot bring herself to be harsh with him.

That afternoon, Tom plays hooky from school, and at supper that night, Aunt Polly tries to trap him into revealing that he skipped school. Tom is able to avert her questioning, until Sid, Tom's brother, squelches on him. Before Aunt Polly can say more, Tom escapes.

Heading into town, Tom meets a stranger, "a boy larger than himself" and—dressed up like a "city slicker." He and Tom get into a fight. Tom gets the better of the other boy and follows him home. The boy's mother appears and calls Tom a "bad vicious, vulgar child" and orders him away. When Tom returns home with his clothes dirty and torn, Aunt Polly decides that, as punishment, he will lose his freedom on Saturday and will have to whitewash the fence.

Commentary

The opening chapter begins dramatically with Aunt Polly frantically calling for "Tom . . . Tom . . . TOM." There can be no child, then as now, who has not heard a parent or guardian calling and has refused to answer; thus, Twain establishes a universal tone in this opening, especially because the caller is established as "The old lady" pulling "her spectacles down" and looking over them for Tom Sawyer.

This opening chapter with four distinct scenes sets the tone for the entire novel. The first scene creates the relationship between Tom and his Aunt Polly. She is a loving spinster aunt who is kind and simple and does not know how to control a young mischievous, strapping lad like Tom but who loves him dearly. "She was as simple-hearted and honest as the day was long, and so she was an easy victim." And thus, Tom takes advantage of her even though he loves her. This scene also reveals Tom's nature. He is the rascally boy out to confound and confuse any adult who tries to repress his youthful nature. He will be seen as quick-witted, full of fun, carefree, and self-willed, but always honorable and fair. This first scene shows these typical characteristics.

The second scene shows Tom playing hooky from school; a typical action for a boy of his age and one that causes him to often receive some type of punishment. Tom's character is developed around these events—the adventures, pranks, and scrapes he enters into willingly or unwillingly—and their consequences.

The third scene establishes the relationship between Tom and his half brother, Sid, a boy as unlike Tom as one can possibly imagine. Tom is the typical "bad boy" of Sunday school lessons who doesn't mind his elders, skips school, and plays tricks on people. Sid is the insipid "good boy" who minds all his elders and does everything expected of him. Sid delights in being a tattletale, in being a prig, and in getting Tom into trouble.

The fourth scene involves Tom's asserting his own turf in the presence of a newcomer, Alfred Temple. The "darings" (I dare you to . . .) and the verbal sparrings lead to a fist fight that Tom wins. Tom is further contrasted to the well-dressed new boy because Tom fights fair while the new boy, when Tom turns his back, cowardly throws a stone and hits Tom.

In short, this first chapter firmly establishes Tom's relationship with his world: He is a child, doing things a child would do. He lives in a slave state. He has no parents, but has a loving, parent figure. And he is mischievous but good-natured.

Glossary

(Here and in the following glossary sections, difficult words and phrases, as well as allusions and historical references, are explained.)

"Spare the rod, and spile the child."   "Spile" is southwestern dialect for "spoil." The saying is attributed by Aunt Polly to the Bible, and the original can be found in Proverbs 13:24: "He that spareth his rod hateth his son: but he that loveth him chasteneth him betimes." The wording that Aunt Polly uses comes from the seventeenth-century satirist, Samuel Butler (1612–1680).

Old Scratch   Another name for the devil.

Evening   Southern and Southwestern for afternoon.

"'NUFF"   A type of contraction for "enough" meaning that the defeated party has had enough of the fight and concedes victory.

Chapter II
The Glorious Whitewasher

Summary

As Tom begins the dreaded task of whitewashing, he sees Ben Rogers approaching. When Ben teases Tom about not being able to go swimming and being forced to work, Tom points out that it is not exactly work if he is enjoying himself, and he makes a great show of applying whitewash and then stepping back to admire his own effects. When Ben wants to try his hand at whitewashing, Tom pretends to be reluctant until Ben offers him first the core of the apple and then the entire apple. Other boys show up—boys who "came to jeer, but remained to whitewash," and by the middle of the afternoon, the fence is whitewashed (by the other boys), and Tom finds himself a rich man, having collected marbles, a part of a Jew's harp, a kite, and many other items as payment from the boys doing the work.

Commentary

In this chapter, Tom reveals his basic knowledge of human psychology; that is, that a person most desires what cannot be easily attained. Tom is also a fine actor, and he cleverly uses this ability in handling his friends. Thus, Tom is able to use this basic understanding of human nature to get others to do his work for him *and* to pay for the privilege of doing it. Instead of being able to join the others at the town center, he brings the center of the town to him, has others do his work for him, and he ends up with all sorts of treasures. In this way, Twain reveals Tom as a natural leader. Throughout the novel, we will see that Tom is the leader; it will always be "Tom Sawyer's gang;" it is always Tom's ideas of what game to play; and Tom is always the winner in games as well as in fights with his peers. He is also usually the winner in his conflicts with the adult world.

The reader is constantly reminded that this is a child's world. Tom tries to make a game out of everything; Aunt Polly's slave, Jim, is fascinated with Tom's sore toe; and Ben Rogers arrives pretending that he is a steamboat on the Missouri River. The wealth or loot the boys offer to Tom is ludicrous and silly and of no worth except to boys of their age.

Note that the occasional and brief appearances of Jim—and other slaves throughout the work—serve to remind the reader that this is slave territory. Slavery never becomes a significant theme in this work—Twain, of course, saved that for *Adventures of Huckleberry Finn*—however the awareness of the slave environment is important.

Glossary

whitewash   a mixture of lime, whiting, size, water, etc., for whitening walls and other surfaces.

white Alley   An alley is a fine marble used as the shooter in playing marbles.

bully taw   An excellent marble. A taw is a fancy marble used to shoot with in playing marbles.

Big Missouri   the name often applied to the Missouri River; also the name of a large steam ship often seen in Hannibal, Missouri.

"labboard" and "stabboard"   Ben Rogers means to say "larboard," the left-hand side of a ship as one faces forward (port) and "starboard," the right-hand side of a ship as one faces forward. His misusage suggests his ignorance of the steamboat.

Chapter III
Busy at War and Love

Summary

In this chapter, Tom first sees Becky Thatcher, although he does not know her name yet. To attract her attention, he begins a series of outlandish and absurd "show-offs" to little avail.

At supper that night, when Aunt Polly is out of the room, Sid accidentally breaks the sugar bowl. Tom is pleased because now the precious Sid will be punished, but when Aunt Polly sees the broken dish, she whips Tom until he points out that Sid broke it. Although Aunt Polly is sorry, she claims that Tom has probably done something deserving of a belting.

Being unjustly accused, Tom thinks how sorry his aunt would be if he were dead and imagines Aunt Polly begging for his forgiveness as he is dying. He works himself up so much that he has to go for a walk, which leads him past the Thatcher house. In his present frame of mind, he wonders if the lovely young girl would mourn his death. He throws pebbles against a window and is drenched by a pail of water being thrown out. Dripping wet, he goes home to bed and skips his prayers. No one except Sid observes this omission.

Commentary

Tom is very clever because he avoids lying to his aunt; instead he merely states that the fence is all finished. He does not say that he painted the fence himself, nor does he let on that others did the work for him. Still, he is quite satisfied to receive not only the rewards for a job well done, but he is able to "hook" a donut while Aunt Polly is not looking.

The mild animosity that develops between Tom and Sid when Sid "squelshed" on Tom now continues as Tom throws some clods at his tattletale half brother. This animosity continues until the last confrontation between the two brothers when Sid reveals the special "secret" of the surprise party at the Widow Douglas' home.

As with many young people who have been unjustly accused and punished, Tom delights in wallowing in his own misery, fantasizing imaginary scenes in which he becomes the suffering martyr. He envisions people feeling guilt and regret for the way they have treated him.

This chapter also introduces the heroine of the novel, Becky Thatcher. Even though the reader does not yet know her name, Twain's description of her and Tom's immediate reaction to her let the reader know that she will be an important part of Tom's young life. Tom's behavior upon seeing Becky for the first time is both exceptionally comic and also very typical of a boy Tom's age. He delights in "showing off" for the pretty new girl, and he exhibits the perfect reactions associated with this youthful love.

Chapters IV and V
Showing Off in Sunday-School; The Pinch-Bug and His Prey

Summary

On Sunday morning, Tom struggles to learn his Sunday school lesson with the help of his cousin Mary, who offers him a present if he can learn the lesson. Tom applies himself and soon has it mastered. On the way to church, Tom swaps items (his wealth from whitewashing) for tickets indicating how many verses in the Bible he has memorized. Tom has collected (bought off) so many tickets that it would appear that he has committed around 2,000 verses to memory—a feat no student has ever accomplished. In Sunday school class, Tom claims the award of a Bible for "knowing" so many verses. Tom is then introduced to Judge Thatcher, who asks him the name of the first two apostles, and Tom blurts out "David and Goliath!"

The monotony of church is broken by a large black beetle that pinches a dog, causing it to clamor up and down the aisles like a rocket. The dog then lands in its master's lap, and the master tosses it out the window.

Commentary

Tom, a very bright boy, has a great deal of difficulty learning his Sunday school lesson because he is bored and "takes no stock" is sermons, not even the famous "Sermon on the Mount." The humor here is that Tom cannot learn the simple verses of the Beatitudes, yet, through his finagling of the red, yellow, and blue tickets, others believe that Tom has memorized over 2,000 verses in the Bible.

True to form, Tom makes a nuisance of himself in Sunday school, pinching, pulling hair, sticking pins into other boys, and committing other annoying acts. Unlike Sid, who is fond of Sunday school, Tom "hate[s] it with his whole heart" and Twain's presentation of a day in Sunday school with the long tedious and boring speeches is proof enough why anyone—except Sid, that is—would dislike it.

Twain is at his best in satirizing religion and church. In the scene with the church service, Twain uses gentle satire to mock and make fun of a typical church service. Consider, for example, the minister who "turn[s] himself into a bulletin-board" by reading long and tedious lists of various meetings, the "little German boy" who recites Biblical verses nonstop and then suffers a nervous breakdown, or the people, such as Mr. Walters and Judge Thatcher, who show up just to be seen or to make an impression. Tom, of course, does the same thing when he barters for the ribbons, which are symbols of accomplishments, not the accomplishments themselves: All the ribbons in the world do not make him know any scriptures.

Also in this chapter, Twain begins to develop an obvious thematic dilemma: Tom's maturation into an adult member of the community, but Twain's disapproval of many of the behaviors found in these adults.

Glossary

Barlow knife   a single blade knife that cost 12 cents.

Doré Bible   an expensively illustrated Bible by the famous French illustrator, Gustave Doré (1833–1883) whose most famous works include illustrations for Dante's *Divine Comedy*.

roundabout   a short, tight jacket or coat formerly worn by men and boys.

"tackle it again"   try to learn the lesson again.

David and Goliath   The story of David slaying the giant Goliath and saving the kingdom comes from the Old Testament. David and Goliath precede the disciples by around 1,500 years.

pinchbug   a type of relatively harmless beetle.

Chapters VI, VII, and VIII
Tom Meets Becky;
Tick-Running and a Heartbreak;
The Pirate Crew Set Sail

Summary

On Monday morning, Tom tries without success to convince Aunt Polly that he is too ill to attend school. His final plea—that his tooth aches—results in Aunt Polly quickly pulling the tooth and sending Tom on his way. On the way to school, Tom meets Huckleberry Finn. Huck is carrying around a dead cat with the intent of taking it to the cemetery that night because he believes the superstition that, when Satan comes to the cemetery to gather the corpses of evil persons, the cat will follow Satan, as will the warts. (In other words, Huck sees this as a way to get rid of his warts.)

Tom arrives at school late and, as punishment, he must sit in the girls' section. He does not mind, however, because the only empty seat is next to Becky Thatcher. Tom draws pictures for her, writes a love note to her, and is so smitten that he doesn't study his lessons and ends up at the foot of the class in a spelling bee. During lunch, Tom and Becky get to know each other, and Tom suggests that they become engaged. Becky agrees, even though she doesn't know what being engaged means. When Tom mentions his earlier relationship with Amy Lawrence, Becky spurns him.

Depressed, Tom plays hooky that afternoon. He thinks of dead Jimmy Hodges and contemplates his own suicide and how sorry Becky will be that she treated him so badly. His solitude is disturbed by his friend Joe Harper, and the two spend the rest of the afternoon playing.

Commentary

Chapter VI is a pivotal chapter because two more of the main characters are presented—Becky Thatcher and Huckleberry Finn.

Character Insight

In spite of their differences, Tom and Huck are good friends and influence each other. Tom is a socially accepted member of society, and Huck is an outcast. Tom lives in a home with a good bed and regular meals and is loved by his Aunt Polly who oversees his physical, emotional, and spiritual needs. In contrast, Huck has no home; is forced to sleep in lofts or hogsheads or wherever he can find a place; must scrounge for his meals, sometimes going without; and has nothing but loose fitting ragged clothes to wear. His only relative, his father (Pap), is the town drunk who is as apt to beat Huck as not. Because of his "freedom"—he has no adult to answer to—Huck is despised and dreaded by the adult community and admired by the youngsters.

Whereas Tom's life is bound by society, by rules, and by acceptable behavior, Huck's life is one of freedom; he can come and go as he pleases. And unlike Tom, Huck's life is uncomplicated. He has no ambition and no desire to be civilized. He hates the idea of respectability and deplores the idea of going to school, wearing proper, tight fitting clothes and cramped shoes, and being forced to do things against his nature, such as giving up smoking and "cussing."

Character Insight

In spite of the differences, Tom envies Huck and Huck's freedom. Tom hates going to Sunday school, and he hates washing. He plays hooky from school, avoids doing chores (such as whitewashing a fence), and envies Huck's free and easy life. Although he seems to aspire to Huck's freedom from convention and rules, Tom is not willing—or able—to truly forgo his conditioning. For example, when Tom has to go into town, he makes up a reason to go alone because he doesn't want to be seen with the disreputable Huck. In this way, there is much of the hypocrite in Tom.

Becky Thatcher is also presented more completely in Chapter VI. Becky is a sweet, somewhat shy girl who has not had a boyfriend before Tom. She is also quick to anger, jealous, and slow to forgive Tom for a supposed wrong. But after some disagreements and after Tom "sacrifices" himself and takes her punishment (these events occur later in the story), Becky and Tom will become devoted friends, especially during the episode in the cave.

Theme

This chapter also presents Twain's use of superstition, a theme that is treated lightly here, but one that gains thematic importance later in the novel. The superstitions become important to the novel because they move the adventures forward. For example, the discussion of how to remove warts leads the two boys to the graveyard at midnight where they witness the murder of Dr. Robinson, and thus create one of the central adventures of the novel.

Glossary

pariah   any person despised or rejected by others; outcast. In reality, Huck Finn does not fit this description, but is so viewed by the members of the town. To the other boys, he is the romantic outcast, someone to be envied.

spunk-water   This could be a variation of "skunk-water," a rank smelling stagnant water found often in rotten vegetation and in tree stumps.

witches and witch detecting   Twain is making fun of the many ways by which a person can theoretically determine whether or not a person is a witch.

hove   heaved or threw.

ferule   a flat stick or ruler used for punishing children.

slathers   a large amount. Tom wants to be a clown in the circus because a clown earn "slathers of money."

zephyr   a soft, gentle breeze.

caitiff   a mean, evil, or cowardly person.

Chapters IX, X, and XI
Tragedy in the Graveyard; Dire Prophecy of the Howling Dog; Conscience Racks Tom

Summary

That night Tom and Huck take the dead cat to the graveyard, where there they hear voices belonging to Muff Potter (the town drunk), Dr. Robinson, and Injun Joe. Dr. Robinson has paid Muff Potter and Injun Joe to dig up the corpse for his medical research. After a fight between the three men, in which Muff Potter is knocked unconscious, Injun Joe stabs Dr. Robinson with Muff's knife. Huck and Tom flee and do not hear Injun Joe convince the drunken Muff that he is the murderer.

Tom and Huck run to the old tannery, where they discuss the dilemma they're in. They both realize that if they reveal Injun Joe as the murderer, he will kill them. The boys take an oath to not reveal what they have seen. Suddenly, they hear a stray dog barking. Thinking it is an evil omen, both boys temporarily renounce their wicked ways.

By noon the next day, the entire town of St. Petersburg knows about Dr. Robinson's murder, and they know that the murder weapon was Muff Potter's knife. School is dismissed for the afternoon, and everyone gravitates to the graveyard, where the sheriff is with Muff Potter, who initially proclaims his innocence. But finally, in despair, Muff tells Injun Joe to reveal the truth. Injun Joe, of course, makes sure that all of the guilt is placed on Muff Potter.

Listening to Injun Joe's lies and machinations, the two boys begin to feel conscience-stricken about their silence. Tom's conscience bothers him so much that he eases it by "smuggling small comforts" to the prisoner, but he can't escape his conscience altogether. At night, he is troubled by wild dreams, and he often talks in his sleep about blood and murder and graves, but his mumblings make no sense.

Commentary

Theme

Superstitions pervade these chapters and mark a new direction that the novel will take. First, superstition is seen in the many sounds that Tom hears and in the various signs that Tom and Huck encounter. At the graveyard, the boys discuss the powers of dead people; they believe that spirits of the dead can hear people talking and can see them in the dark. This discussion leads to the various superstitions connected with the entire Injun Joe episode.

Until this point in the novel, Twain has shown the childhood adventures of Tom and some of his friends to be all innocent fun. That is, Tom is the mischievous boy playing various types of pranks, creating great adventures using pirates and robbers, and fighting great wars. Furthermore, Tom has been seen in terms of his relationships at home, at school, at Sunday school, and at play with his friends. In this chapter, there begins a simple adventure in the graveyard concerning a dead cat. This adventure, however, is vastly different from anything that Tom or Huck have previously confronted. In the person of Injun Joe, Tom and Huck have their first encounter with pure evil. They witness first a grave robbery, then an argument, and finally a fight that ends in a murder.

Character
Insight

Two new characters are also introduced in this chapter: Muff Potter and Injun Joe. Muff Potter is the town's disgrace—a drunk and worthless person who is hired to help dig up the corpse of the recently buried Hoss Williams. Muff is not very bright and is easily persuaded by Injun Joe that he is the murderer. Muff's trust in Injun Joe indicates his simple-mindedness. After the murder, Potter is depicted as fearful, weak, hopeless, confused, and literally shaking, partly from alcohol and partly from fear. The townspeople take advantage of his weakness and willingly believe Injun Joe; they condemn Muff Potter on the basis of rumor and hearsay even before any formal accusation is made against him.

Character
Insight

In contrast, Injun Joe is a vicious, wicked, and evil man. The murder of Dr. Robinson is not the first murder that he has committed, and he later has no compunction about mutilating Widow Douglas. He is the personification of evil, and his evil is seen in his willingness to kill a man for revenge or for some trivial reason. The townspeople are willing to believe Injun Joe because they are afraid of him and fear retaliation from him. Thus Huck and Tom are right in their fear of Injun Joe. Future chapters show Tom and Huck helping Old Muff Potter and being deeply frightened by Injun Joe.

Literary Device

Twain's literary artistry is seen in the techniques he uses to depict Injun Joe. He never comments directly on Injun Joe's evil. Instead, he shows how evil Injun Joe is by the boys' reaction to him. Here are two boys in the cemetery at midnight: Thoughts of dead people don't scare them. Thoughts of ghosts don't scare them. Even thoughts of the devil don't scare them. But they are pushed to panic by the presence of Injun Joe. Their reaction to his presence is more effective than a straightforward statement of his evil would be.

In this chapter, the two boys flee from the murder scene, "speechless with horror." They are confronted with real evil and with the realization that if they tell, their lives will be in jeopardy. This situation contrasts dramatically with their make-believe adventures in which death is an exciting—and imaginary—prospect. To protect themselves, the boys agree to remain silent, and they make a complicated ritual of this oath-taking, a ritual that involves both writing out the oath and signing it in blood—a technique that Tom has learned from the books he has read. Taking this blood vow later makes Tom reluctant to reveal the truth.

In these chapters, Tom's world has suddenly reversed itself. The days of happy childhood pleasures and adventures are gone: Aunt Polly does not scold him as usual; instead she weeps over him, which is much more upsetting. At school, Tom is flogged for playing hooky the preceding afternoon, but he hardly notices the punishment because his mind is occupied with the horrors of the preceding night. And, when Becky returns his brass doorknob, his world of childhood innocence is temporarily brought to an end.

Glossary

"All the old graves were sunken in." A reference to the fact that a mound over the grave meant that a new coffin has just been buried and the displaced soil mounded up over the coffin.

lugubrious very sad or mournful, especially in a way that seems exaggerated or ridiculous.

Chapter XII
The Cat and the Pain Killer

Summary

When Tom finds out that Becky Thatcher is ill, he puts aside all of his interests and involvements, as well as his fear of Injun Joe. Aunt Polly notices this drastic change in his behavior and, thinking him ill, gives him a dose from one of her favorite cures. Tom's melancholy disappears, and he perks up immediately. Tom enjoys the medicine so much that he pesters his aunt for another dose. She finally tells him where it is so that he can administer it himself. While doing so, Tom gives the family cat a taste, and the cat spreads "chaos and destruction" everywhere.

Later, when Tom sees Becky at school, he performs all sorts of antics to attract her attention, but she ignores him.

Commentary

This chapter acts as an interlude between the Injun Joe murder plot and the future plot involving the boys on Jackson's Island.

With the episode about the painkillers, Twain returns to telling wonderful anecdotes. Regardless of what the pain might be, all nineteenth-century quack medicines (or patent medicines, for that matter) had one quality in common: They were about 90 percent pure alcohol. Although these medicines had no therapeutic or medicinal values, they at least made the patient feel less pain. In the case of Tom and the cat, the medicine made them feel elated, joyous, and rambunctious. Of course, they were drunk.

Glossary

inveterate to be addicted to or to become a habit.

balm of Gilead anything healing or soothing.

Chapters XIII and XIV
The Pirate Crew Set Sail; Happy Camp of the Freebooters

Summary

Feeling forsaken and friendless and like a "boy . . . [whom] nobody loved," Tom decides to turn to a life of crime. He meets Joe Harper, "his soul's sworn comrade," and they begin to lay their plans and decide to include Huck Finn as a member of their gang of pirates. Huck, having no qualms about which life of crime is the best, readily agrees, and the three plan to meet that night.

When they meet at the appointed place, each boy identifies himself by his assumed pirate name; then they "borrow" (or capture) a small log raft to take them to Jackson's Island where they make camp. The following afternoon, the boys hear an unusual sound—a "deep, sullen boom came floating down out of the distance"—and see a ferry crowded with townspeople. Tom realizes that "somebody's drowned." After spending a few moments wondering who, the boys realize that the townspeople think *they* have drowned. All three are excited and over-joyed at the thought that they are the center of attention and will be the envy of all of their companions. When Joe vaguely hints that maybe they should go home because of the grief their families must be feeling, Huck and Tom ridicule him. When Huck and Joe go to sleep, however, Tom writes two notes; he leaves one note in Joe's hat; he keeps the other note and wends his way to the sandbar.

Commentary

The reasons for the escape to Jackson's Island are varied. Tom feels depressed and dejected because of Becky Thatcher's rejection of him. Joe Harper's situation is similar: He is depressed because his mother punished him for throwing out some cream—a crime of which he is innocent. (Later, in fact, his mother will despair after Joe is "dead" because she remembers throwing out the cream herself.) Like Tom, Joe wants to escape "civilization," but he is also the first to tire of the island

and the first who wants to return to his family. For Huck Finn, who has no responsibilities and no one to notice that he is gone, one place is as good as another.

Character Insight

Each boy assumes a pirate name, and these names come from books that Tom has read. Twain makes a subtle, albeit important contrast from the natural common sense intelligence of Huck Finn to the acquired fanciful ideas that Tom Sawyer gets from his books. Tom, for example, has idealized ideas about what pirates look like and how they act—based on the various books that he has read. Tom shares his knowledge of pirates (gained from his book reading) with the other boys. He explains how pirates capture and burn ships, take and bury treasure, and kill the men and carry the women away to their island. When Tom points out that pirates also wear gaudy clothing and gold, silver, and precious jewels, Huck looks at his rags and faces the reality that he "ain't dressed fit for a pirate."

The first day on the island is one of the most glorious days in the boys' lives, one lived to the fullest. But at night, Tom and Joe, who have basically the same upbringing, have guilty consciences over stealing food for the outing. Even though they say their bedtime prayers (something Huck would never bother with), their consciences do not let them sleep. Their conscience is an ironic contrast to their boastful talk of capturing ships, stealing, killing men, and kidnapping women. In contrast, Huck Finn has no pangs of conscience. He feels no qualms about having lifted (stolen) certain items; he feels no compunction to live by the rules of a society that has made him an outcast. He has had a marvelous day because he is getting more to eat than he usually gets in the village. For Huck, this life on the island is an idyllic existence, especially since neither he nor Tom have any thoughts of the grim aspects of the grave robbery and the murder of Dr. Robinson. On this island, there is no feeling of terror and no talk of superstitions.

When Tom awakes the next morning, he feels himself at one with nature; he thrills merely watching the antics of birds and even insects. When Huck and Joe awake, their day is filled with natural joys and contentment; a sense of quiet joy pervades their lives—"here was a delicious sense of repose and peace in the deep pervading calm and silence of the woods." The realization that their raft has floated away makes them realize that they have truly escaped from society and are isolated and abandoned. Twain has thus presented the perfect life. However, soon the sounds of thunder turn into cannon fire and the mood drastically changes. A ferryboat descends upon them, bringing the society from which the boys have escaped. When the boys realize that the ferryboat is searching for them—everyone believes they have drowned—they initially like the idea of being cried over and of causing suffering to those who have been mean to them. It is not long, however, before Tom and Joe are concerned because they know how their families must be are grieving. Huck, who has no family, does not share this concern.

Chapter XIV ends with Joe wanting to return home only to be talked out of it by Tom. Tom himself waits for his friends to sleep and he quietly slips away, and the chapter ends with this mystery.

Chapters XV and XVI
Tom's Stealthy Visit Home; First Pipes—"I've Lost My Knife"

Summary

Tom sneaks back to his house in St. Petersburg and overhears Aunt Polly making plans for his funeral. Aunt Polly commiserates with Mrs. Harper (Joe's mother), both agreeing that the boys were "mischievous . . . giddy . . . and harum-scarum" but they never meant any real harm. Both women regret that the last things the boys heard from them were reprimands. Although tempted to dash out and reveal himself (the theatrical nature of such a revelation appeals to him), Tom restrains himself. Instead of leaving the note as he planned, Tom leaves with the note still in his pocket and returns to the island where he, Joe, and Huck continue their adventures. Eventually, Joe Harper becomes homesick and, despite Tom's ridicule, he starts home. Huck, who has no home, also desires to return to his customary haunts. After all else fails, Tom reveals to them his secret plans, and the other boys decide to remain.

That night, the boys are awakened by an approaching, driving storm. They take shelter under the inland tent until the tent blows away. Then they huddle together under an oak tree. After the fierceness of the storm abates, they return to their camp and find it destroyed. They realize that could have been killed had they remained in their camp.

Commentary

Chapter XV presents Tom's journey back to the village. The fact that it takes all night and is physically an arduous trip suggests something of Tom's physical maturity and his mature ability to undertake such a venture. The main import of the chapter is Tom's overhearing Aunt Polly and Mrs. Harper discuss his and Joe's disappearance along with Mary's good words and Sid's attempts to say something negative. Hearing himself praised as being a basically good but mischievous person, Tom "began to have a nobler opinion of himself." He wants to reveal himself but "the theatrical gorgeousness of the thing appealed to him."

As the scene continues, Tom is emotionally drained by Aunt Polly's grief, but he still constrains himself.

In this scene, Twain has Tom hide in order to overhear a conversation about himself. This technique was often used in dramas at the time. Traditionally, the character would hide behind a screen and listen to the conversations of others; hence, such scenes were called "screen scenes." Chapter XV fits into this category.

Tom's concern and love for his Aunt Polly is seen in the fact that he makes the trip into the village to leave her a note telling her that he is safe. His love for the theatrical, however, and his anticipation of his dramatic return to life, overshadow the more humane concerns for her grief. Here, the thoughtlessness of youth and Tom's selfish desire for amusement at the expense of the genuine grief of his Aunt Polly are difficult to understand.

After Tom returns to the island, the three boys live an idyllic life that consists of fishing, hunting, and playing games. In this way, Twain creates an idyllic picture of the world of young boys, a world longed for and dreamed about, a world of carefree, imaginative play—and a world that cannot last. This idyllic world is, literally in this chapter, the "calm before the storm." After having presented the peaceful, sunny days of an ideal existence, the calm is shattered by the storm. The fear the boys feel is evident as they cling to one another; that their fear is justified is evident in the destruction and havoc that the storm causes to their temporary camp. The contrast between the wild storm and the peaceful, sunny days shows that even an idyllic spot can be dangerous and harsh.

The difference between Tom and his friends clearly shows why Tom is always the leader of the group. Joe is the first to express his dependence on this family and wants to return home. Even Huck, who has no home, misses his old haunts and agrees with Joe. Thus Tom is the leader who constantly encourages Joe and Huck when they are lonely, suggesting new games to play and finding new occupations for them.

Glossary

Yawl a small, two-masted sailing vessel usually manned by four to six oarsmen and used for duties for which a larger vessel could not maneuver.

knucks, ring-taw, and keeps   types of games played with marbles.

Six Nations   the five Indian nations (Mohawks, Oneidas, Onandagas, Cayugas, and Senecas as a group) of the Iroquois confederacy plus the Tuscaroras.

Chapters XVII and XVIII
Pirates at Their Own Funeral; Tom Reveals His Dream Secret

Summary

It is a tranquil Saturday afternoon in St. Petersburg, but there is no gaiety as the adults prepare for the boys' funerals. Becky Thatcher finds herself moping about the schoolyard, feeling very melancholy. She has nothing to remember Tom by, and she wishes she had the brass knob that she returned to him. On Sunday, the toll of the church bell calls the mourners to the funeral services. The eulogies begin, noting the rare promise of the lost lads, their sweet generous natures, their noble and beautiful actions, and their promise.

Suddenly, "there was a rustle in the gallery" and with the creaking of the door, the entire congregation rises and stares at the three boys alive and walking down the aisle, first Tom and then Joe followed by Huck in his "drooping rags." Aunt Polly smothers Tom with affection; she even embraces Huck Finn. The minister leads the congregation with hymns of praise. For the rest of the day, Tom receives more "cuffs and kisses" than he has received in a year.

At school, Tom has become a great hero, and the young children follow him about in a sort of adoration. Tom and Joe are both envied and admired by their peers and they become conceited and swaggering. Tom decides that fame and "glory" is quite enough for him and he doesn't need Becky's attention any more. When she arrives, he ignores her and pours special attention on Amy Lawrence. As Tom did earlier, Becky now tries to get Tom's attention by showing off, by inviting other children to her picnic. As Tom continues to ignore her, Becky decides to make Tom jealous and she seeks out the company of Alfred Temple.

Now, in spite of glory, Tom finds himself tormented, especially because he finds Amy's chattering and nonsense intolerable. At noon, Tom goes home because he does not want to see Becky enjoying Alfred's company. Becky soon becomes tired of Alfred, especially since Tom is not around to suffer, and she sends him on his way. For his part, Alfred realizes that he has been used, and, for revenge, he pours ink over Tom's book at the passage for the day's lesson. Becky glances into the school-room in time to witness Alfred's treachery, but she decides to let Tom be punished because of the way he treated her earlier.

Commentary

These two chapters involve difficult questions appropriate to all humorists. That is, can a superb joke be a good one when it involves such intense suffering as Aunt Polly and Mrs. Harper endure? At what point does the comic element or the joke become one of bad taste. As a vibrant youth, Tom does not understand the true suffering he has caused: As is often true, he is more concerned with his own pleasures at the expense of adult feelings.

The great scene with the appearance of the boys alive at their own funeral is heightened by the many regrets of various characters: Becky is sorry she kept no memento of Tom and wishes she had retained the brass knob he had given her. The townspeople regret that they had not seen the potential of each boy. All Tom's playmates recall the last time that they had seen Tom. The funeral orations are undercut by the mourners' hypocrisy—that is, after the supposed death of the young boys, the boys are praised for the very things in life for which they were condemned. All of these feelings are placed in the background in con-trast to the dramatic and theatrical gesture of the boys walking down the aisle alive and healthy at their own funeral. It is not until the next day that Aunt Polly, while admitting that it was "a fine joke," also expresses her suffering and grief and wonders if Tom really cares for her at all.

These chapters continue to develop the idea that "the course of true love never did run smooth." While Becky had mourned for Tom, now Tom, basking in his own fame and many attentions, pretends to ignore her, and Becky performs all the silly antics to get Tom's attention that Tom had earlier performed to get her attention. Her desire for revenge is seen when she decides to let Tom take the blame for the spilled ink on his spelling book. Later, however, Becky will fully redeem herself when she and Tom are lost in the cave.

Chapters XIX and XX
The Cruelty of "I Don't Think"; Tom Takes Becky's Punishment

Summary

That noon, Aunt Polly immediately accosts Tom for lying to her. She has visited with Mrs. Harper (whose son Joe had told her everything) and found out that Tom had actually been over that night and overheard everything that he pretended was in a wonderful dream. In addition to Tom's lying to her is the humiliation she suffered from being made a fool of: "It makes me feel so bad to think you could let me go to Serena Harper and make such a fool of myself and never say a word."

Tom admits that his actions were mean, but he didn't intend to be mean; instead, he came over, he tells her, to let her know that she should not be uneasy about him. Aunt Polly believes it is another lie, but Tom is earnest that he came only "to keep you from grieving." Aunt Polly wants to believe him but is still cautious. Tom explains that when he heard them planning the funeral, he thought of the fun it would be to suddenly walk in and surprise everyone. This is the reason he didn't leave the note on the bark. Aunt Polly is surprised about the note, and after she sends him back to school, she goes to the closet to check his clothes. After vacillating back and forth about whether she should check for the note, she eventually does. Finding it, Aunt Polly's confidence in Tom's basic goodness is restored.

The scene with Aunt Polly encourages Tom to make up with Becky, and when he approaches her, she strangely rejects him and stomps away. He is confused by the incomprehensible actions of girls. Becky, meanwhile, has seen Alfred pour the ink over Tom's spelling book but decides not to tell so that Tom will receive a whipping.

While Becky is wandering about the classroom, she sees that Mr. Dobbins' top desk drawer is open. In it is a book on anatomy, which he reads when the class is busy with projects. All the students are completely entranced about the nature of the book, and Becky has the perfect opportunity to find out what the book contains. She looks about and, seeing that no one is around, removes the book with its handsome engraved and colored frontispiece and finds "a human figure, stark naked." At this moment a shadow falls across her book: It is Tom Sawyer. In her rush to conceal the book, she tears one of the pages. Now she is horrified because this offense will warrant a whipping in front of the entire class. She blames Tom and hurries from the room. Tom thinks a little licking isn't that important and decides to "let her sweat it out."

When school begins again, the ink spots on Tom's spelling book are revealed. Tom is accused and whipped, even though he stoutly proclaims his innocence. Ironically, Becky is not as happy as she thought she would be, and has to repress an impulse to inform on Alfred. She justifies her silence by assuming that Tom is going to reveal her guilt about the anatomy book.

Later in the afternoon when all are busy, Mr. Dobbins removes his book and discovers the torn page. When he asks the class who tore the book, no one volunteers, so he begins to question each student. When he reaches Becky Thatcher, she turns her head away, and when Mr. Dobbins orders her to look him in the face, Tom springs to his feet and says, "I done it."

Mr. Dobbins administers the most merciless flogging that he can. Tom, however, is consoled by the look of adoration in Becky's eyes. After the beating, he is forced to remain two hours after school, but he doesn't mind because he knows that Becky will be waiting for him. And, indeed, she is. She tells him of Alfred's treachery and her abetting it, but only her words, "Tom, how COULD you be so noble," have any lasting meaning for him.

Commentary

Tom's character might be summed up in the statement that he makes when Aunt Polly chastises him for lying to her and, more important, letting her make a fool of herself in front of Mrs. Harper: "Auntie, I know now that it was mean, but I didn't mean to be mean. I didn't. Honest." His statement reflects the universal thoughtlessness and inconsideration that such youths have for the adult. Rather than detract from Tom's total worth, it merely confirms that his actions are those of most early adolescents. And to Tom's credit, he does acknowledge that his good joke now looks mean and shabby.

Even Aunt Polly would readily admit that the whole scheme had a certain flair and imagination about it and that, if she had not been the principal sufferer concerned, she could have laughed at the entire plan. Nevertheless, the simple truth remains that she was very hurt and frightened by this practical joke, regardless of its mastery. Her hurt is deepened by Tom's lying to her and allowing her to look foolish in the eyes of Mrs. Harper. She does, however, check out Tom's statement, and finding the note written on the bark, she knows again of Tom's basic goodness and love for her.

During the nineteenth century, it was a very common practice to use a paddle or some other instrument in order to whip children. Although boys were whipped frequently, young girls were virtually never whipped. Knowing this fact increases the horror of what Becky faces if it is revealed that she tore the anatomy book. Not only would it have been a horrible ordeal for Becky, who is basically sweet, to be beaten, but it also would have been a disgrace for her family. Tom's actions—accepting the blame for the torn page and taking the beating in Becky's place—redeem his character and are best summarized by Becky's simple statement "Tom, how COULD you be so noble."

The two incidents concerning the spilled ink on the spelling book and the torn page in the prized anatomy book make a parallel contrast to the earlier scene in which Tom hurt his Aunt Polly: Tom is falsely accused of spilling ink on his spelling book, and Becky could have easily saved him, but she remains silent. In contrast, Tom could have let Becky take her deserved punishment, but he cannot bear to have her distressed and humiliated; therefore, he nobly takes her punishment for her. In this contrast, Tom is seen as more kind and less spiteful than Becky.

Chapter XIX functions partly to make Tom aware of Becky's actions. Feeling contrite for how badly he has treated his Aunt Polly, he is able to return to school and offer an apology to Becky for ignoring her and her picnic. Chapter XX presents the further estrangement between Becky and Tom. By the end of Chapter XX, however, everything is resolved between them, and we are ready for the later cave scene where the two youths will be lost together.

By following this chapter (The Cruelty of "I Don't Think") with the next (Tom Takes Becky's Punishment), Twain contrasts Tom's thoughtlessness in the first with his sacrifice for Becky Thatcher in the second.

Chapter XXI
Eloquence—The Master's Gilded Dome

Summary

With the end of school and vacation approaching, the schoolmaster, Mr. Dobbins, is determined that his students will make a good showing in the school's final examination. Thus he is very liberal in the use of the rod and other punishments. He is very faithful in whipping the younger students vigorously, frequently, and effectively. The smaller boys rack their brains for some suitable revenge against Mr. Dobbins' excessive floggings. They conceive of a wonderful plan, and they swear the sign-painter's boy into their plot because the schoolmaster boards at his father's house.

The night set aside for a display of learning arrives, and the school hall is lavishly decorated. Everyone in the town is present. The little folk recite their pieces with great difficulty, pleased only to get it over. The highlight of the night is the reading of original compositions by some of the older girls. Each theme is extremely melancholy, filled with cliches and trite pronouncements. The winner is "A Vision," a dreadfully gushy, melancholy piece with no originality.

Now is the time for revenge. The schoolmaster, who has been nipping from his bottle of private reserve liquor, is a little unsteady on his feet, and as he tries to draw a map of the United States, the audience begins to twitter. From above him in the attic, a cat is being slowly lowered through a trapdoor directly above his head. As soon as the cat can reach it, the cat snags the schoolmaster's toupee, revealing his bald head, which had been gilded gold by the sign painter's son and which shone like a star.

Commentary

This delightful chapter, filled with irony, sarcasm, and satire, has little or nothing to do with Tom Sawyer except that Tom was probably among those who were punished.

With the girls' essays—filled with melancholy—Twain pokes fun at the tender sentimentality of the average person and the popular literature of the day. He is satirizing the average person's preference for cheap, morbid writing that has no literary value. Instead of this melodramatic claptrap, Twain would prefer a simple straightforward essay.

This chapter also presents a realistic picture of the typical country school and a delightful episode about the students' revenge on the schoolteacher, which involves the cat, Mr. Dobbins' wig, and finally his bald head painted gold by the sign painter's boy. This scene serves as another example, like the Sunday school scene in Chapter IX, of Twain's satirizing authority figures.

Chapter XXII
Huck Finn Quotes Scriptures

Summary

Tom admires the uniforms of the Cadets of Temperance and joins them so that he can strut at the funeral of Judge Frazer, who is dying. When the Judge has a turn for the better, Tom resigns from the Cadets of Temperance, but then the Judge has a relapse and dies. The funeral is a fine thing, but Tom is free from it. He attempts a diary, but nothing comes of it. He attends a minstrel show, and he and Joe play minstrel for two days. A senator comes, but he is not impressive. A circus comes and leaves the next day, so the boys play circus for a while and then abandon it. A phrenologist and a mesmerizer come, and still the boys are bored and dreary.

Then Tom has the measles for two weeks. He is better for a short time and then has a relapse that lasts three weeks. Between the two bouts with measles, all his friends get religion—even "Huck quoted some scripture!"—but by the end of the second bout, all is normal again.

Commentary

Style & Language

As with Chapter XXI, the purpose of Chapter XXII is not so much to move the story along, but to show the boredom that pervades during vacation in a small town. Twain presents this boredom by showing the boys trying one type of amusement and then quickly changing to another type. The significance of both these chapters is that Tom's life—any child's life, in fact—can be common and boring. During the summer months, so anxiously awaited, the boys feel an isolation and loneliness that they do not necessarily feel during the rest of the year. In other words, tedium is worse than school.

Making matters worse for Tom, Becky is away on vacation; thus he struggles to find things to do. For this reason—and because he is attracted to their fancy uniforms—Tom joins the Cadets of Temperance. He soon drops it, however, and picks up something else to occupy him for a time. The irony is that Tom wants to wear the showy uniform; however, the cadets are only wearing the uniforms because the judge is dying. When the judge doesn't die, there is no need for wearing the uniform and thus, Tom quits.

Literary Device

In many of his writings, Twain pokes fun at organized religion, and he takes the opportunity to do so again here. With Tom and his friends, Twain points out the superficiality of religious revivals. In the nineteenth century, religious revivals were a common occurrence in the summer. Here, all the boys "got religion"—momentarily, at least.

After the interludes of these two chapters, Twain returns to his main plot line.

Chapters XXIII and XXIV
The Salvation of Muff Potter; Splendid Days and Fearful Nights

Summary

At last, the day of Muff Potter's trial arrives. It is the sole absorbing story of the entire town. Every report about the trial makes Tom shudder, and he finds Huck Finn in order to reassure himself that Huck has told no one. Huck tells Tom that he will tell only when he decides that he wants Injun Joe to drown him, for he knows that they will not be alive for two days if they reveal what they know. The boys then swear again not to reveal the truth because the consequences of their telling would be tantamount to their own deaths.

Tom and Huck discuss the rumors going about town and how it is obvious that Muff Potter will be convicted and executed. Then they remember certain little favors that Muff had performed for them and agree that Muff is basically a harmless drunk who has never done anyone any mischief; he is certainly not the hardened villain that he is depicted to be by the village.

The boys do as they have often done before: They take various items, such as tobacco, to Muff's jail cell, and they try to comfort him. Muff tells the boys how kind they are and remembers all of the good things about them. Tom and Huck leave feeling guilty and miserable.

At the first day of the trial, the prosecutor presents evidence and witnesses that point to Muff as being the murderer, and the defense attorney does not cross-examine. Even the townspeople are dissatisfied that the defense attorney is simply "throwing away his client's life without an effort." Tom and Huck have avoided going into the courtroom. That night, Tom is out very late.

The next day, after the closing remarks of the prosecutor, the defense attorney changes his plea; surprisingly, he calls Tom Sawyer to the witness stand and asks where Tom was hiding on the night of the murder. Tom can hardly answer but finally reveals that he was hiding only a few feet away from the murder scene. Then, in his own words—and by now

Tom is speaking freely—he describes the entire scene. When Tom reaches the climax of the story, Injun Joe jumps through the courthouse window and escapes. Upon Tom's revelation, the fickle town, which had openly condemned Muff Potter, now takes him "to its bosom."

Once more, Tom is the "glittering hero" and the envy of every boy in the village. While Tom's days are ones of exultation and praise, his nights are horrors. His dreams are nightmares, and he will not leave home after dark. While Huck's name was never mentioned in court, Huck is still afraid that word of his involvement will get out, because his "confidence in the human race was well-nigh obliterated." Rewards are offered for Injun Joe, and a fancy St. Louis detective arrives and leaves, but Injun Joe is not found. After some time, Tom's fears abate somewhat.

Commentary

Character Insight

The basic goodness of the two boys is revealed in their concern about the fate of Muff Potter. When they recall all of the little things that Muff has done for them, their consciences are aroused, and they conclude that actually Muff is a simple, harmless person who would never hurt anyone. Yet in spite of their consciences, they know that if they tell, they will both be dead within a short period of time. Thus weighing everything, they again renew the pledge never to tell.

The entire trial is centered upon Tom's reactions; Huck does not even attend the trial, but rather, he waits outside the courtroom. During Muff Potter's time in jail and throughout much of the trial, all the evidence seems to prove Muff Potter's guilt, and, until the last day of the trial, Tom's chief concern is for his own safety.

Character Insight

In this chapter, however, we see Tom's moral integrity emerge. During the course of the trial, Tom sees justice being perverted, and he, of course, recognizes the evil—and guilt—of Injun Joe. Although he is still frightened to reveal the truth, Tom begins to change. Then he mysteriously disappears at night, and it is not until later that Twain lets the reader know of Tom's whereabouts. When Tom is called to the witness stand, we realize that Tom has revealed to Muff Potter's defense lawyer what he witnessed in the cemetery on the night of the murder. On the witness stand, in spite of the real danger to himself, Tom bravely tells the truth. This is his most mature, heroic, and courageous action.

The trial scene is presented almost entirely from Tom's point of view. Through his eyes, we see Muff Potter as pale, weak, haggard, and hopeless. In fact, Tom had considered helping Muff escape, but he knows it would be useless because the man is too incompetent and would be caught immediately. In contrast to the weak and pathetic Potter, Injun Joe is a confident man of action. When Injun Joe realizes that he has been identified as the murderer, he wastes no time; he simply escapes as rapidly as possible.

Huck has also matured, but in a different way. Until Tom broke his solemn oath and testified in court, Huck had implicit faith in the value of oaths. Now, however, he is completely disillusioned, and his faith in the efficacy of oaths is shattered. In fact, his belief in the honesty and integrity of human beings in general is destroyed; he is now completely disillusioned, but he has become less gullible and more mature.

Conceivably, Tom's maturity is complete with his testimony against Injun Joe; his adventure, however, has not reached a climax.

Chapters XXV and XXVI
Seeking the Buried Treasure; Real Robbers Seize the Box of Gold

Summary

There comes a time in every boy's life when he feels the need to dig for buried treasure. Feeling this need, Tom tries to round up his companions but can find only Huck Finn, who is available for any adventure. Tom explains in detail all the distinctions and subtleties of finding buried treasures—mysterious maps and instructions, proper "haunted" places and where to look for them, and what to do with the immense fortunes. Huck claims he will spend his fortune on eating and enjoyments because his "Pap" will take it all from him when he finds out about it. Tom is more conventional; he will save some of the fortune for a marriage.

The boys hike into the forest, and after digging several holes and finding no treasure, they decide that they must wait until midnight. They hide their tools and plan to meet at midnight [a bewitching hour] and dig under a special tree behind Widow Douglas' house. They meet at the appointed time and begin digging at the end of the shadow cast by the moonlight at midnight, thus signifying the presence of buried treasures. After an hour, Tom again decides that they are digging in the wrong spot. They decide to dig at a haunted house that no one ever goes around, but because they are not at ease with dead folks, ghosts, and supernatural events such as strange blue lights coming from the house, they decide to do their digging in the day time.

At noon the next day—Friday the 13—the boys start out for the haunted house fully aware of the dangers on this particular date. Furthermore, Huck has had a bad dream about rats, which is a sure sign there is trouble. To avoid bad luck, Tom and Huck spend that afternoon playing Robin Hood instead.

On Saturday, the boys meet again at the haunted house on Cardiff Hill. After digging a bit, they decide to go into the haunted house.

Peeking inside, they sense something "weird and grisly about the dead silence," and there is an aura of isolation and desolation. After examining the downstairs, they venture upstairs together and look around.

As they are about to descend, Tom and Huck hear voices downstairs. They see one of the men: He is the old deaf and dumb Spaniard who has been seen around town a few times. When he begins to talk, the boys recognize him as Injun Joe in disguise. They do not recognize the other man. The two men discuss plans for another robbery, and Injun Joe mentions a revenge he must perform. Although Injun Joe and his companion eat and then fall asleep, the boys are too afraid to attempt an escape.

By and by, Injun Joe and his companion awake and decide to bury a packet of about six hundred silver coins that they have stolen. While digging a hole, they discover a metal box filled with gold coins worth thousands of dollars. Eventually, the men leave with their treasure, which they plan to hide in Injun Joe's "den number two."

Tom and Huck decide to keep a sharp lookout for the "Spaniard," and after he has completed his "revenge," they will follow him to his hiding place. Then they suddenly realize that the revenge is against them—at least against Tom.

Commentary

The opening sentence of Chapter XXV expresses the universal truth that sometime in the life of every boy there comes a time when he wants to search for buried treasure. This sentence leads to a continuation of the adventure that began in the graveyard and that runs throughout the plot of lesser adventures. That is, it propels the boys toward the inevitable confrontation with Injun Joe. This sentence also leads Tom and Huck to the discovery of the existence of buried treasure, the episode within the cave, and the discovery of the treasure itself.

When Tom explains the nature of buried treasure, he demonstrates his "book learning" and his love of the theatrical or romantic. When the boys discuss how they will spend the money, Huck Finn is the more realistic one: He wants to spend it all immediately on enjoyment because his pap (father) might hear of it and come back and take it all away from him. Tom, however, will spend some of the money on "fun things" but wants to save a large portion of it to use for things such as his marriage, thus indicating a more mature outlook.

The theme of superstition is reintroduced in these episodes. The boys are superstitious of Friday the 13; they believe treasure can only be found at the bewitching hour of midnight; they feel that a horrible dream about rats is dangerous; and they are aware of "signs" such as a haunted house, a skull, witches, dead people, blue lights, and ghosts that will affect their finding treasures.

At the haunted house, the two boys have an unexpected adventure that endangers their lives. Injun Joe had disappeared quite some time ago, but now Huck and Tom recognize that the Old Spaniard is actually Injun Joe. And although they do not know the other vicious man in rags, they are fearful of him. What started out as a game no more serious than playing pirates, Indians, or Robin Hood, now becomes a serious and dangerous situation. The boys are fully aware that they are in the presence of a murderer who hates them and would have no qualms about killing them.

The boys overhear a conversation while hiding and discover that Injun Joe has a secret hiding place which he calls "den number two." When the villains find the buried gold and Injun Joe realizes that someone is upstairs, he takes the gold with him. Thus, this scene is directly correlated to the scene in the cave when Tom catches sight of Injun Joe's hiding place and is later able to find the gold treasure.

Glossary

hy'roglyphics   a picture or symbol representing a word, syllable, or sound, used by the ancient Egyptians and others instead of alphabetical letters.

serape   a brightly colored, wool blanket, used as an outer garment by men in Spanish-American countries. Here it is used by Injun Joe to disguise his identity.

Murrell's gang   a band of robbers that roved a part of the frontier and gained only minor recognition.

Chapters XXVII and XXVIII
Trembling on the Trail;
In the Lair of Injun Joe

Summary

The next morning, Tom seeks out Huck to reaffirm that the money and the adventure they experienced the day before is real. He and Huck discuss how they will find "den number two." Tom discovers that "Number Two" is lived in by a young lawyer, and that the other "Number Two" is a room in the Temperance Tavern which is kept locked except late at night. Tom decides that he and Huck will take all the keys they can find and, on a dark night, see what is inside the "Number Two" at the Temperance Tavern. If either sees Injun Joe, he is to follow him in the hopes of discovering the hiding place.

On a dark night, Huck stands guard while Tom tries the Temperance Tavern door. Suddenly, Tom comes running down the alley, calling to Huck to follow him. They take refuge in a slaughterhouse just as a tremendous rainstorm begins. Tom explains his fear: The keys wouldn't work, but the door opened when he tried the doorknob. Stepping inside, Tom almost stepped on Injun Joe's outstretched hand: The half-breed was passed out on the floor with an empty bottle of whiskey beside him. Tom suggests that they go back and look for the cache of gold coins, but Huck is more practical: If there were three empty bottles of whiskey instead of only one, maybe he would go back, but now Injun Joe might wake up after only one bottle of whiskey.

The boys decide not to try the room again until Injun Joe is gone. They make arrangements for Huck to watch at night; during the day, he can sleep in Ben Roger's hayloft. Tom and Huck also decide not to disturb each other unless something important happens.

Commentary

The plot of the buried treasure continues to occupy Huck and Tom. Again, Tom's character stands in contrast to Huck's: Tom treats the whole adventure as a fanciful dream such as he often has. Huck however does not dream of the treasure but more realistically, he thinks of Injun Joe's killing them.

For the third time in the novel, Twain uses a thunderstorm to express the boy's fears: In the first instance, he used a storm at Jackson's Island to express the dangers and fears of the boys out camping. In the second, a rainstorm follows Tom's measles to reflect the anxieties that Tom has undergone. Here, the storm in the slaughterhouse reflects the possibility of the boys' own murders.

Twain enjoys using any occasion to make fun of hypocrites and hypocritical behavior. The Temperance Tavern, by its name, is not supposed to have any alcoholic beverages; but instead it has a large storage room filled with various types of alcoholic beverages. As Twain has often suggested, there are many people who swear temperance in church on Sunday only to follow it with a drunken spree on Monday.

Tom adheres to social mores. For example, in this chapter, while Tom enjoys Huck's company, he does not want to be seen with him in public places. Huck, outcast that he is, also exhibits this same propensity to adhere to certain mores of his time. For example, even the lowly Huck does not want it to be known around town that he has actually "set right down and eat with him [Uncle Jake, a black servant]. But you needn't tell that. A body's got to do things when he's awfully hungry he wouldn't want to do as a steady thing." (Interestingly, in *Adventures of Huckleberry Finn*, Huck travels down the river on a raft with the escaped slave, Jim, and risks his life—and his soul—for Jim's sake.) Readers should remember that Twain wrote in the nineteenth century when slavery still existed. Consequently, his characters conform to the prejudices of the time.

Glossary

hogshead   a large barrel or cask holding from 63 to 140 gallons (238 to 530 liters).

Chapters XXIX and XXX
Huck Saves the Widow;
Tom and Becky in the Cave

Summary

Tom hears good news on Friday morning: The Thatcher family has returned from their family vacation. Tom spends most of the day with Becky, and she talks her mother into the promised picnic for the next day.

Invitations are sent out, and everyone gathers the next morning for the chartered ferryboat. Mrs. Thatcher decides that, because it will be late, Becky should stay with a friend near the ferry landing. Tom talks Becky into joining him for ice cream at the Widow Douglas' house after the ride, and Becky reluctantly agrees.

Three miles down river, the ferry boat stops, and everyone plays until someone shouts that it is time to try McDougal's cave, a "vast labyrinth of crooked aisles." Everyone knows some of the cave—and Tom knows as much as anyone did—but no one alive knows the entire cave. After much wandering about, the group finally leaves the cave to discover that it is almost dark, and the ferryboat is anxious to make the trip home.

That night, while Huck watches "Number Two," the door opens, and two men brush past him. Because he does not have enough time to give Tom Sawyer the signal, Huck carefully follows the men, who go to the quarry. When the men stop, Huck hides and listens. He overhears Injun Joe planning revenge: Some years earlier, Judge Douglas, Widow Douglas's late husband, had Injun Joe horsewhipped in public. To get even, Injun Joe plans "to slit [the widow's] nostrils and notch her ears like a sow."

The two men see a light in the Widow's house and, thinking that she has company, decide to wait until later in the night. Huck silently creeps away and runs frantically to the Welshman's house, which is close by. He tells what he has heard and makes the Welshman and his sons promise not to tell who told them. They all leave for the sumac bushes with Huck lingering behind. When he hears shots, he waits no longer and runs back to town as quickly as possible.

As soon as it is daylight, Huck goes back to the Welshman's house. The Welshman is glad to welcome Huck into his house because of Huck's courage and because he prevented the Widow from being mutilated. Huck hears how the Welshman and his sons hid behind a spot in the sumac bushes and were only fifteen feet away from Injun Joe when an unfortunate sneeze came upon the Welshman. The robbers ran away. The Welshman and his men fired after them and pursued Injun Joe and his partner, but the men escaped capture.

Huck explains to the Welshman how he had seen the two robbers and had followed them and overheard them talking about mutilating the Widow Douglas' face. Under pressure, he reveals the identity of Injun Joe, and the Welshman promises to protect him from this vicious man. A loud knock at the door causes Huck to jump almost out of his skin. It is the Widow Douglas and a group of citizens who want to express their gratitude to the Welshman. Mr. Jones (the Welshman), in turn, tells the widow that "There's another that you're more beholden to . . . but he don't allow me to tell his name."

At church that morning, Mrs. Thatcher discovers that Becky is missing. Shortly after that, Aunt Polly discovers that Tom is also missing. The people realize that they are still in the cave. Two hundred men are gathered, and they immediately go to the cave to begin the search. On Monday, the many men return, and Huck is found sick with a high fever. The Widow Douglas comes to care for him. When Huck hears a discussion about the Temperance Tavern break-in, he jumps up from his fever and asks if anything had been found. He is told that only whiskey had been found. When he asks about Tom Sawyer, they keep Tom's disappearance from him.

The search for Tom and Becky continues for three days. They find a hair-ribbon and the children' names lettered on the wall—proof that they are still in the cave. Despair settles in when the men no longer have either hope or energy to keep looking.

Commentary

These two chapters describe the various activities of the entire group in the cave, and the return home, then abruptly change to a narration about Huck Finn's adventures in town.

Twain does not return to Tom and Becky's adventures in the cave until Chapter XXXI, but the reader must remember that both Tom and Becky are in the cave with its many passageways and unknown areas.

Although the reader is not aware of it yet, this is the scene of Tom's most perilous adventure and the only one that involves Becky Thatcher. Earlier, Mrs. Thatcher had arranged for Becky to stay with the Harper family, and as a result, Becky and Tom are not missed until church the following morning.

Character Insight

With Tom in the cave, we see Huck Finn acting on his own. Until this point, we have only seen Huck in relation to Tom, and when Tom is around, Tom is the leader of the two. He is the one with the education; he is also the one who is a respected member of society and the one who is expected to know what should be done in any situation. Huck has always been agreeable to Tom's suggestions and leadership, and he does what Tom wants him to do. However, now that Huck in on his own, we see that he is naturally smart, shrewd, and resourceful.

Huck's following Injun Joe to the hideout is a dangerous and frightening task, but he follows the two men carefully and overhears their plan to mutilate Widow Douglas' face, tie her up, and in other ways harm her. Huck's integrity cannot allow this. However, because he is not welcomed in the homes of the townspeople, he goes to awaken the Welshman, Mr. Jones, and tell him what he has heard. Thus, we see Huck doing the "right thing" in protecting the Widow Douglas because he is both fond of her and does not wish to see her hurt. This leads to the Widow's desire to protect and take care of Huck.

Huck's reception and welcome by the Welshman, Mr. Jones, is the most kindness and attention he has ever received, and Huck is not insensitive to this kindness. After the Welshman and his sons have chased Injun Joe away and when Huck returns early the next morning to discover the result—that is, what could have happened to the treasure—the Welshman greets him by commenting that the name of Huck Finn can "open this door night or day . . . and welcome." Huck cannot remember ever hearing the word "welcome" by anyone before and is deeply pleased with such kind treatment. Likewise, when he becomes ill, the Widow Douglas comes to care for him because of her own innate kindness. The reader should remember that she does not know at this time that it was Huck who saved her life. Here and elsewhere, Twain begins to be more interested in the character of Huck Finn—his native intelligence and his good moral sense. In fact, Twain's treatment of Huck in *Tom Sawyer* foreshadows the later novel, *Adventures of Huckleberry Finn.*

Injun Joe's evil and wicked nature is again emphasized. He so strongly feels the need of revenge that he will take out his evil hatred on an innocent person.

Chapters XXXI and XXXII
Found and Lost Again;
"Turn Out! They're Found!"

Summary

In the cave, Tom and Becky wander around with the others for a while, and then they meander off by themselves. Seeing some other places, Tom plays at being a discoverer and investigates new paths with Becky following him. They find wonderful natural stairs, waterfalls, springs, stalactites, and finally, they run into some bats from which they flee, failing to mark their whereabouts. They try to find their way out and can't. First Tom and then Becky realize that they are lost. Becky falls to the ground and cries while Tom tries to comfort her by telling her it is all his fault.

They begin to wander again, hoping to find a familiar landmark. Tom takes Becky's candle and blows it out to conserve that source of light. After a while, Becky has to sit down, and she falls asleep. When she awakens, she and Tom stumble on until they find a spring: Tom explains to Becky that they must stay close to water because their candles are almost gone. They are both very hungry, and Tom shares a piece of cake that he had saved from the picnic. Suddenly, Becky realizes that her mother will think she is spending the night at the Harper's house and that they won't be missed until sometime Sunday. They sleep again and then share the last bite of the cake. Suddenly, they hear voices in the background. The two begin shouting, but to no avail, and the sounds fade away.

Tom decides to explore side passages, leaving Becky sitting by the spring. At the end of one corridor, he sees a human holding a candle; he shouts loudly and to his horror it is Injun Joe. The shouting has also frightened Injun Joe, who runs away. After some time, Tom is so hungry and Becky is so weak that he leaves her and explores other passages. Becky feels that she will now die, and she makes Tom promise to return to her soon and hold her during her final moments. Acting as bravely as he can, he leaves her to try to find an exit.

Three days have passed, and the villagers are in mourning for the loss of Becky and Tom. Mrs. Thatcher is ill, and Aunt Polly is distraught. Then "in the middle of the night, a wild peal burst from the village bells" and there were shouts: "Turn out! turn out! they're found! they're found!" A messenger goes to the cave to inform Judge Thatcher, who is still searching.

Using all types of exaggerations and embroidering the story as much as possible, Tom tells of his and Becky's wonderful adventure. He thoroughly enjoys the attention of the people who listened intently to his every word.

Three days and nights in the cave have drained the strength of both Tom and Becky; Tom gets better in three days, but it takes a week for Becky to regain her strength. Meanwhile, Tom has heard of Huck's illness, and he visits him, but the Widow Douglas refuses to allow Tom to tell about his awesome adventure in the cave. Tom does hear that the ragged man was found drowned in the river while trying to escape. About two weeks later, Tom goes by to visit Becky. Judge Thatcher tells him that he has had the cave locked and secured so that no other children can get inside. "Tom turned as white as a sheet" and explains that "Injun Joe is in the cave."

Commentary

The true importance of this chapter is Twain's narration. The reader is very concerned over the fate of Becky and Tom, and we experience all of the fears and dangers that they face. Twain is able to make the threat of their starving very real, and we sense the hunger in the manner in which they greedily eat the piece of picnic cake, knowing that there is no more real food except the bit that Tom nobly saves from his share. The appearance of Injun Joe in the cave ties together the murder scene in the graveyard, the discovery of the gold treasure, and the location of the treasure. In addition, it adds suspense to the episode.

In these episodes, Tom's character rises to new heights. He is mature in protecting Becky; he is noble in his concern for her because her welfare is of utmost importance to him; he takes full blame and responsibility for their predicament; and he even tries to encourage and bolster her sagging spirit. In contrast to his youthful behavior earlier, he now conducts himself in a mature and truly admirable manner. Our esteem for Tom grows still further when we see his reaction to learning that Injun Joe has been trapped in the cave. While he has dreaded and feared Injun Joe and even though he recognizes the evil within Joe, Tom's reaction is one of horror when he discovers that another person, even the despicable Injun Joe, is trapped as he and Becky had been trapped.

Likewise, Becky rises in our estimation. She had earlier been seen as a petulant, spoiled, somewhat selfish girl, and she had allowed Tom to take her punishment. Now she refuses to blame Tom for their situation and shares in the blame. She does not question Tom's judgments, and she faces her death calmly.

Glossary

stalactite   an icicle-shaped mineral deposit, usually a calcium compound, that hangs from the roof of a cavern and is formed by the evaporation of dripping water that is full of minerals.

Chapters XXXIII and XXXIV
The Fate of Injun Joe;
Floods of Gold

Summary

After discovering that Injun Joe has been locked in the cave, a large party of townspeople go to McDougal's cave to search for him. Tom is in the forefront of the party. At the closed door of the cave, they find Injun Joe's body with his "bowie-knife" close by. He had tried to cut through the door, and although he probably realized the futility of this endeavor, he kept cutting as something to do while he starved to death.

Although Tom feels sorry for Injun Joe's suffering, he also feels a great sense of relief and freedom from the fear that he has felt since Injun Joe escaped from the trial in which Tom testified against him.

Injun Joe's funeral is a festive occasion: People from all the neighboring towns come to witness it. The next day, Tom and Huck have a long talk. Huck then tells Tom all about his adventures on Cardiff Hill but says that he doesn't want his part in the events to be known because Injun Joe might have left friends who would enact revenge against Huck. Tom then announces that the treasure is somewhere in the cave. The boys make plans to retrieve it.

After gathering their supplies and "borrowing" a skiff from "a citizen who was absent," Tom leads Huck to the opening that he and Becky escaped from. The passageway is so concealed that Huck is standing almost on top of it and cannot see it.

After hours of digging and finding nothing, Tom remembers that the treasure is *under* the cross, so they dig again and soon find the treasure box, which is too heavy to carry. The boys divide the treasure into bags and then load their treasure into the skiff and return to the village. There Tom borrows a wagon, and the boys pull the treasure as far as the Welshman's house, where they stop to rest. The Welshman, Mr. Jones, comes out and helps them pull the old "metal" to the Widow's house where a party is in progress. Huck is fearful about going in, but Mr. Jones insists. Everyone of importance is at the Widow's house, and she takes the boys upstairs to the bedroom, instructs them to wash, and shows them new clothing to put on before they come downstairs.

Left alone, Huck's first impulse is to climb out the window. Sid appears and tells them that the Widow Douglas is giving the party for the Welshman (Mr. Jones) and his sons for saving her from Injun Joe and his companion. Sid explains that it is supposed to be a surprise party because the Welshman is going to reveal Huck's heroic actions in saving the Widow, but he maintains that everyone already knows about it. Tom is disgusted with Sid because he knows that Sid is the person who has told everyone and ruined the surprise, and he kicks him out and dares him to tell Aunt Polly.

At the party, the Welshman gives a little thank you speech and reveals that it was really Huck Finn who was responsible for saving Widow Douglas. The Widow tries to look surprised and tells Huck that she has already made plans for him to live with her, go to school, and eventually open up a small business for himself.

Tom Sawyer then blurts out the surprise of the evening: "Huck don't need [money]. Huck's rich." Thinking that everyone is laughing at him, Tom runs out the door, brings in the treasure, and pours it on the table, saying that half is his and half belongs to Huck. The spectacle of so much gold money lying on the table leaves everyone speechless. Tom explains how they came about the treasure, and when counted, it amounts to over twelve thousand dollars.

Commentary

Upon the discovery on Injun Joe's body, the reader gets another glimpse into Tom's compassion. In spite of the horrors that Injun Joe had caused him, Tom's personality allows him to sympathize with Injun Joe's plight because Tom had been in the same situation: "Tom was touched, for he knew by his own experience how this wretch had suffered." It is Tom's human compassion even for this dreadful specimen of humanity that endears him to the reader.

The death of Injun Joe in Chapter XXXIII brings one significant part of the novel to an end. Injun Joe played an important part in Tom's growth, as well as Huck's. First, Tom and Huck witnessed the murder committed by Injun Joe. Until that point, for Tom at least, all adventures had been excitingly imaginative. The events in the graveyard mark his first *real* adventure. At the trial of Muff Potter, Tom matures enough to bring the truth to light and convict Injun Joe of murder, thus freeing the innocent Muff Potter. When Injun Joe reveals his plans to mutilate the Widow Douglas, Huck, who until that point has been primarily motivated by fear for his own life, puts that fear aside to save the Widow Douglas. As a result of Injun Joe's crimes, both boys have matured tremendously—Tom in his testimony and Huck in following Injun Joe to Cardiff Hill and thus saving the life of the Widow Douglas. In essence, Tom matures as a young man; Huck gains a place in the society, as signified by the Welshman's befriending him and the Widow taking him in.

Chapter XXXIV also prepares the way for a new life for Huck Finn. It is almost as though Twain had already conceived and thought out a novel dealing with the adventures of Huck Finn, a novel he would actually spend much of the next eight years writing.

Glossary

lucifer matches   These were the then newly invented friction matches with the standard phosphorus compound on top which could light by striking it on some solid material.

orgies   Tom misuses the word to mean having a big Indian-type "pow-wow" or celebration.

Chapter XXXV
Respectable Huck Joins the Gang; Conclusions

Summary

Tom and Huck's discovery of buried treasure changes the entire village: Everyone now seeks out old haunted houses and digs in vain for buried treasure. The Widow Douglas invests Huck's money at 6 percent, and Aunt Polly has Judge Thatcher do the same for Tom. This is wealth, a dollar a day for every weekday and half a dollar on Sunday at a time when "a dollar and a quarter a week would board, lodge, and school a boy . . . and clothe him and wash him, too, for that matter."

Judge Thatcher "has conceived a great opinion of Tom" for getting Becky out of the cave. Thus when Becky tells her father about Tom's taking the blame for Becky's misconduct and taking her punishment, the judge claims that "it was a noble, generous, a magnanimous lie."

Huck Finn finds wealth a burden. He has to dress properly, eat at a table with a knife and a fork, and sleep in a clean bed. More horrible, Huck has to quit smoking and swearing. In other words, he has to live a sterile, boring, and civilized life, and so he disappears. Three days later, Tom finds him in a hogshead behind a slaughterhouse, dressed in his old loose-fitting clothes and smoking. Huck tells Tom that he cannot stand civilization; he feels too crushed. Even the new tight-fitting clothes smother him; school is about to open, and he does not want to go to school.

Tom tries to convince Huck that all the things Huck objects to are the things that the other boys have to endure. Nothing convinces Huck until Tom tells him that he cannot join his band of robbers unless he is respectable. Huck, Tom continues, cannot have a place in the gang because people would say "Sawyer's Gang! Pretty low characters in it!" And they would be referring to Huck Finn. Huck then promises that he will return to the Widow's for a month and will follow most of her rules if Tom will get her to ease up a little bit on him. They look forward to getting the gang started, and plans are made for a swearing-in ceremony that will be performed with real blood and on top of a coffin.

Twain declares his novel finished and describes Tom's status at the same time: "So endeth this chronicle. It being strictly a history of a boy, it must stop here; the story could not go much further without becoming the history of a man." And so the novel ends.

Commentary

At the end of the novel, Tom asks Huck to shed his ways and become a member of society, that is to become respectable. Society is Tom's way of life, and he does not want to escape from it except in his childhood games of pretend. Huck, however, foreshadows the Huck of *Huck Finn*, a fourteen-year-old person who has tried society and has rejected it. (Interestingly, Twain ends *Adventures of Huckleberry Finn* in much the same way: There, again, Huck wants to escape from the confining rules and hypocrisy of society in favor of a life of adventure and freedom.)

Literary Device

Tom, in contrast, is preparing again for his make-believe world. In this make-believe world, Huck Finn cannot become a member of Tom's band of robbers unless in the real world he becomes respectable. The irony escapes Tom, but is apparent to the adult reader—a fact that again shows this novel's appeal to both children and adults, alike.

The ending of *Tom Sawyer* served Twain as a jumping off point for his next novel, which he would not complete for another eight years: *Adventures of Huckleberry Finn*. It is as though he had discovered his favorite character in Huck, a person who lived apart from normal society and who, from the perspective of an outsider, would be able to criticize it.

CHARACTER ANALYSES

The following critical analyses delve into the physical, emotional, and psychological traits of the literary work's major characters so that you might better understand what motivates these characters. The writer of this study guide provides this scholarship as an educational tool by which you may compare your own interpretations of the characters. Before reading the character analyses that follow, consider first writing your own short essays on the characters as an exercise by which you can test your understanding of the original literary work. Then, compare your essays to those that follow, noting discrepancies between the two. If your essays appear lacking, that might indicate that you need to re-read the original literary work or re-familiarize yourself with the major characters.

Tom Sawyer

As the title of the novel suggests, Tom Sawyer is the central character of the novel. Tom appears in almost every scene as the chief character. The one major exception occurs when Tom and Becky are lost in McDougal's Cave and the focus of the novel switches to Huck Finn's search for Injun Joe.

Central to Tom's character is his age. Twain deliberately did not specify his age. For many readers, Tom's age fluctuates from scene to scene. Most readers like to view Tom's age as approaching puberty—around eleven or twelve years old. If he were younger, he would not be so interested in Becky Thatcher. His fondness for Becky, while still marked by his youth (turning somersaults and otherwise acting foolish to get her attention, passing "love notes" back and forth in school, and so on), exhibits a caring and maturity that goes beyond only "puppy love." Consider, for example, his protective attitude toward her when he took the blame and punishment for her and how he cared for her in the cave episode.

Tom's character is a dynamic one, that is he moves from enjoyment in the most famous of boyhood games—playing "Indians and Chiefs," pretending to be Robin Hood, and so on—to actions that require a high degree of moral integrity. Consider, for example, his highly moral decision to break the boyish oath he took and to reveal Injun Joe's guilt in murdering Dr. Robinson—an act that freed an innocent man and placed Tom, himself, in jeopardy.

If we view *Tom Sawyer* simply as a boyhood adventure story, then we must assume that Twain viewed Tom erratically and used many episodes from his own youth at different times over a long period of time. Thus we have two Toms: one who plays boyish pranks on his Aunt Polly—"hooking" an apple or doughnut when she is not looking, teasing her, and finding ways to get around her—and one who has the maturity to save an innocent man and protect a frightened girl.

However, if we view Tom Sawyer as a tale of maturing, a *bildungsroman*—a novel whose principal subject is the moral, psychological, and intellectual development of a youthful main character—then we don't see two Tom's but one who, through his experiences, matures as a young man. Most readers then choose to see Tom as a dynamic character who occasionally reverts to childish pranks, but one who essentially moves from early childish endeavors and, when called upon to do so, matures to the point where he can make highly moral decisions and commitments, as he did in revealing Injun Joe's guilt and in protecting Becky while lost in the cave.

Injun Joe

Next to Tom Sawyer, Injun Joe is the most important character in the novel. During a boy's maturation, he must sometimes encounter evil in its most drastic form, and it is through Tom's reactions to Injun Joe that we most clearly see Tom's growth from a boy into a young man.

Injun Joe is a thieving, dishonest, wicked person who achieves most of his evil goals because he is also clever and resourceful. He kills young doctor Robinson without qualms and for no discernible reason except for pure evil pleasure. He frames old Muff Potter, and he is shrewd enough to make the townspeople believe his story is true. When proof of his part in the murder is about to be revealed, he reacts quickly and decisively at the trial: He takes immediate action and jumps out the window and escapes and cannot be found by the search parties. In addition, his reputation is such that none of the citizens will confront him with his evil. Although all the citizens of St. Petersburg know that he is evil, each is too frightened to confront him because they, like Tom and Huck, know that he will retaliate in a violent manner.

Injun Joe is a static character, that is, he is the same at the end as he is in the beginning. He does not change through the course of the events in which he is involved. He is the essence of evil when we first see him murdering Dr. Robinson and framing Muff Potter for the crime, and he remains the essence of evil throughout. Consider, for example, his plan to mutilate the Widow Douglas in retaliation for something her late husband did years earlier.

Injun Joe is central to the novel's primary adventure and appears in some of the most important scenes in the novel: He is first seen murdering Dr. Robinson and framing the innocent Muff. He flees justice at Muff Potter's trial. He is the central figure in the search for buried treasure; he shows up, disguised as a deaf and mute Spaniard, in a haunted house where Tom and Huck are hiding upstairs. Later, he displays his extreme cruelty as seen in his plans to revenge himself on the Widow Douglas. When he threatens to kill his partner if the latter refuses to help him mutilate Widow Douglas, he simply reinforces his evilness. Tom encounters Injun Joe in the cave, where he is finally trapped with his ill-gained gold and dies a befitting but horrible death.

Huck Finn

The adults look upon Huck Finn as a disgrace and as a bad influence upon their sons and daughters. The youngsters look at him with envy because he has complete freedom to do whatever he likes. His only living relative is his father (Pap) who is the town drunkard and absent most of the time. When Pap is present, he uses Huck as a punching bag. Huck has no formal education; therefore, he looks to Tom and his book-learning as superior in intelligence to his own common sense. He admires Tom's fanciful notions about how to play games and readily joins in and is content to let Tom be the leader while he himself plays the lesser parts.

Huck's only clothes are the worn-out rags that others have discarded and that seldom fit him. He lives without bathing except in the Mississippi River during warm weather, has no bed to sleep in, and no regular food—only that which he can obtain by his own wits. He does not attend school or church, and he has no regular chores to perform. Because he is completely free to do anything he likes, boys admire him, and all the boys enjoy his company.

Although Tom is the central or most dynamic character in the novel and the one who changes the most, we should not dismiss the change that occurs in Huck Finn. Huck is an outcast, and he conducts himself as an outcast. Until Mr. Jones the Welshman invites and welcomes Huck into his home, Huck has never been invited into anyone's house. He is realistic, knowing that he does not belong. Because he exists on the periphery of society, Huck's character acts as a sort of moral commentator on society—a role he resumes in Twain's great American masterpiece, *Adventures of Huckleberry Finn*.

Nevertheless, when the outward layers and superficial forms of society are stripped away, the reader sees another dimension of Huck's character revealed. Near the end of the novel he proves his nobility when he risks his own life to protect the Widow Douglas, and unlike the typical boy, he does not want praise or recognition. Nevertheless, Huck is very uncomfortable living in a decent house, sleeping in a good bed, wearing decent clothes and shoes, eating good food, and not being allowed to curse, swear, or smoke.

Huck is centrally involved in the Muff Potter story, the Jackson's Island adventure, and the story of Injun Joe and the treasure. And it is he who stops Injun Joe from mutilating the Widow Douglas. These final actions win the admiration of the community that had earlier spurned him.

Becky Thatcher

Becky is not a well-developed character. Instead she is the symbol of the beautiful, unapproachable girl—"a lovely little blue-eyed creature with yellow hair plaited into two long tails, white summer frock and embroidered pantalettes." Her striking looks capture Tom immediately. Yet even though she is not a fully developed character, her influence on Tom Sawyer is immense, and it is this outward effect on Tom that is important. Tom's attraction to Becky is one of the charms of the novel. It is the typical case of puppy love and infatuation. It exposes the more mature side of Tom's character.

Becky is very pretty, proud, and jealous, and she seems to appreciate Tom's devotion only after he allows himself to be punished in her stead. When she and Tom are lost in the cave, however, we see that she is not strictly a static character, that is one who never changes. To the contrary, Becky is indeed worthy of the affections that Tom showers on her. Although fearful of death in the cave, she fully trusts Tom and does not blame him for their terrible predicament. She actually shows more courage and stamina than the reader would have expected under the circumstances as she faces death with a serene bravery.

CRITICAL ESSAYS

On the pages that follow, the writer of this study guide provides critical scholarship on various aspects of Mark Twain's *The Adventures of Tom Sawyer.* These interpretive essays are intended solely to enhance your understanding of the original literary work; they are supplemental materials and are not to replace your reading of *The Adventures of Tom Sawyer.* When you're finished reading *The Adventures of Tom Sawyer,* and prior to your reading this study guide's critical essays, consider making a bulleted list of what you think are the most important themes and symbols. Write a short paragraph under each bullet explaining why you think that theme or symbol is important; include at least one short quote from the original literary work that supports your contention. Then, test your list and reasons against those found in the following essays. Do you include themes and symbols that the study guide author doesn't? If so, this self test might indicate that you are well on your way to understanding original literary work. But if not, perhaps you will need to re-read *The Adventures of Tom Sawyer.*

Tom Sawyer and Huckleberry Finn: A Study in Contrasts

Tom Sawyer and Huck Finn are the two most well-known characters among American readers. In fact, one could say that they are the most famous pair in all of American literature. Tom and Huck are completely different from each other in nearly every way. In fact, they are polar opposites in basic living situations and in the ways in which they view the world.

Lifestyle

While Tom and Huck share the common bond of being orphans, Tom lives in a civilized household with an aunt who loves him, who is tolerant of his boyish pranks, who is indulgent with his youthful escapades and whims, and who is deeply concerned about his welfare. In contrast, Huck Finn is alone, has no home, and his father is the town drunkard who completely ignores his son and, in his drunken rages, beats him violently. Thus, Huck has no one to take care of him. It is a sad commentary indeed that, at the end of the novel, Mr. Jones is the first adult ever to welcome Huck inside a private home.

While Tom sleeps in a comfortable bed at night, Huck might be found sleeping in someone's barn, in a cardboard box, or his favorite sleeping place, in an empty hogheads barrel. In fact, this is where Tom finds him after one of their episodes. And while Tom is served three meals a day, Huck has to scrounge for food for himself. Their clothes are vastly different; Tom is dressed as a typical schoolboy would be dressed, but Huck wears discarded overalls held up by one buckle, and he most often goes barefoot.

Tom goes to the accepted and respectable school, attends Sunday school, and is invited to parties in other people's homes. Huck does not attend school and, naturally, is not invited to parties. Instead he is free from responsibility and moves freely in and out of the town, sometimes disappearing for days, and is never missed. His education is from the proverbial "school of hard knocks."

In contrast to Tom, Huck is an outcast from society. Rather than conform, Huck thrives on his freedom from such restraints as society imposes. He cannot abide by the strictures of living in a regular household where there is no smoking and no cussing and where he must wear proper clothes, keep decent hours, and conform to proper manners, especially table manners. Whereas Tom's life is bound by society, by rules, and by acceptable behavior, Huck's life is one of freedom; he can come and go as he pleases.

This difference between Tom and Huck is seen on Jackson's Island. The first day on the island is one of the glorious days in their lives, one lived to the fullest. But at night time, Tom and Joe, who have basically the same upbringing, have guilty consciences over stealing food for the outing, and even though they say their bedtime prayers—something Huck doesn't bother with—their consciences will not let them get to sleep. In contrast, Huck Finn has no pangs of conscience. He feels no qualms about having lifted (stolen) or borrowed certain items; he feels no compunction to live by the rules of society that has made him the outcast that he is. In fact, Huck has had a marvelous day because he is getting more to eat that he usually gets in the village.

Outlook on Life

Tom is filled with imaginative schemes, but they all come from adventure stories he has read. Tom makes everything seem fancy and "high faluting." He adds extra touches so as to give the simplest undertaking an air of magic, and he conforms rigorously to the rules—as he interprets them—from the fancy works of fiction he reads. Huck is not a reader, but instead he possesses a mind capable of performing feats that would escape Tom's bookish imagination. Tom is a dreamer, and Huck is always the practical or pragmatic person.

Unlike Tom, Huck's life is uncomplicated. He has no ambition, no desire to be civilized. He hates the idea of respectability and deplores the idea of going to school, wearing proper fitting clothes and cramped shoes, and being forced to do things against his nature, such as quitting smoking and not "cussing."

As a member of society, Tom knows the bounds and limits of that civilized society and adheres to its rules and limitations. Of course, he is full of pranks and wild schemes, but always in the back of his mind are the rules of society which he obeys. Yet there is much in Tom that is hypocritical. For example, when he has to go into town, he makes up a reason to go alone because he does not want to be seen with the disreputable Huck.

Huck, who is an outcast, is not constrained by society's rules as Tom is. Instead, Huck's decency is innate rather than learned.

How They Perceive Each Other

Tom envies Huck's freedom. As noted earlier, Tom hates going to church; Tom hates going to Sunday school; and he hates washing. He plays hooky from regular school, avoids doing chores (such as whitewashing the fence—note that Huck is *not* among those conned into doing Tom's work), and envies Huck's free and easy life. Ironically, the very boys—including Tom—who long for Huck's freedom and are envious of Huck's lifestyle could not survive under Huck's conditions.

As Tom envies Huck's lifestyle, Huck admires Tom's book-learning and sees Tom as a standard of civilized behavior. When Tom explains how pirates dress, Huck doesn't question his knowledge. Just as the other boys do, Huck admires Tom and willingly follows him.

Ultimately, Tom is the conformist to society and its restraints while Huck is the outcast, the individualist, the free soul who cherishes his own freedom.

Tom Sawyer: The Movie, the Musical, and the Novel

As popular as the novel is, there has never been a commercially successful film made from it. Furthermore, no movie version of *Tom Sawyer* has ever captured the essence of the novel. Many TV films have attempted to capture the unique qualities of the novel but have, for the most part, failed, partly because the novel appeals on two such different levels—that of the adult and that of the child. Perhaps the most successful (and most easily obtained) version is *Tom Sawyer*, produced by Panavision Films in 1973, which stars Johnny Whitaker as Tom Sawyer, Jodie Foster as Becky Thatcher, and Celeste Holm as Aunt Polly.

The purpose of comparing two such different approaches to a single work is that by doing so, we can more easily see the problems of transferring a story from one medium to another, and in evaluating the changes from one medium to another, we come to a better understanding of the original work.

Like a Broadway musical comedy, the movie begins with an overture and then shows a still picture of the Mississippi River. This shot is accompanied by a musical overture composed by the famous John Williams, winner of many awards for best musical score.

At the beginning of the movie, we hear the school bell ringing and we see Tom Sawyer leaving home, hiding his books, removing his shoes and running barefooted through the town, and arriving at the river's edge where he meets Huck Finn and Muff Potter. Immediately, the person who has read Twain's novel recognizes that this work is different. Huck becomes a central character in the movie (thus his appearance in the opening sequence).

Also, the character of Muff Potter becomes central to the film. Unlike in the novel, the film's Muff assumes the central comic role: Throughout the movie, he is constantly discovering whiskey in some strange place where he has previously hidden it. Instead of being introduced late in the novel and then only at the graveyard performing an illegal act, he is a central part of the movie. We hear of the plot in the graveyard immediately as Injun Joe, mean and fierce looking, tells Muff that Dr. Robinson is looking for them. This introductory scene ends with Tom and Huck playing on a raft in the middle of the Mississippi River to the accompaniment of music.

From the opening scene to the end, the movie takes equal liberties with the novel to the point that one could not identify the movie as based on Twain's novel *The Adventures of Tom Sawyer* except for the similarity of the title. Readers of the novel will recognize, for example, other points of difference:

- The differences between Tom and Huck are not explored. In fact, they are minimized.

- The role of Mrs. Harper is expanded to included the role of the Widow Douglas, a change which adds nothing significant to the movie.

- Many of the minor scenes are missing from the movie, and while critics may argue over the relevance of these minor scenes, they are nevertheless memorable to the reader.

- Although the movie captures the fun of the whitewashing episode, the purpose of the scene is lost. Instead, it becomes a major musical production, splendid but artificial and thin.

- Because the movie is a joyous celebration of youthful exuberance and happiness, there is no place for the gruesome death of Injun

■ At the end of the movie, Tom and Judge Thatcher are on a river-boat, leaving Hannibal for a visit down river, and Tom spies Huck alone on a raft on the Mississippi River.

Essentially, the movie is a colorful extravaganza with lots of pretty scenes, youthful exuberance, and good dancing and music (albeit without any notable or memorable songs). In its broadest outlines, the movie picks up bits and pieces of the novel but possesses no real significant meaning. It is a bit of fluff best seen when one wants to escape from reality.

CliffsNotes Review

Use this CliffsNotes Review to test your understanding of the original text and reinforce what you've learned in this book. After you work through the review and essay questions, identify the quote section, and the fun and useful practice projects, you're well on your way to understanding a comprehensive and meaningful interpretation of *The Adventures of Tom Sawyer*.

Q&A

1. When Tom Sawyer sees the new girl in town with her pretty blonde curls, he ceases to think about _____.

2. When Tom and Huck are in the cemetery, they witness the murder of _____.

3. Muff Porter is innocent of the murder but is framed by _____.

4. The first and only person ever to welcome Huck Finn into his home is _____.

5. At the end of the novel, Injun Joe is found dead in _____.

6. Huck and Tom discover _____ gold dollars in the cave.

7. Tom's cousin _____ promises him a Barton knife if he takes a good bath for Sunday school.

8. Huck promises to become a conformist and live with the Widow Douglas if he can join Tom's _____.

Answers: (1) Amy (2) Dr. Robinson (3) Injun Joe (4) The Welshman [or Mr. Jones] (5) McDougal's Cave (6) $12,000. (7) Mary (8) Band of Outlaws, or Robbers

Identify the Quote: Find Each Quote in *The Adventures of Tom Sawyer*

1. He had discovered a great law of human action, without knowing it—namely, that in order to make a man or a boy covet a thing, it is only necessary to make the thing difficult to attain

2. The widder eats by a bell; she goes to bed by a bell; she gits up by a bell—everyting's so awful reg'lar a body can't stand it

3. We can't do that . . . We can't let you into the gang [of robbers] if you ain't respectable

4. Why that ain't anything. I can't fall; that ain't the way it is in the book. The book says . . .

5. I tell you again, as I've told you before, I don't care for her swag [money]— you may have it. But her husband was rough on me—many times he was rough on me—and mainly he was the justice of the peace that jugged me for a vagrant . . . He had me *horsewhipped!* — with all the town looking on! . . . He took advantage of me and died. But I'll take it out of her

Answers: (1) The narrator comments on Tom's ability to analyze human nature and to exploit it for his own good. Whereas Tom's knowledge most often comes from his books, here his native intelligence is illustrated. (2) Huck, upon having been adopted by the Widow Douglas, laments the loss of his freedom. (3) Tom informs Huck that only "respectable people" can belong to his exclusive band of imaginary robbers. Tom does not see any contradiction in his ironical statements and thereby creates the humor of the statement itself. (4) In speaking to his friend Joe Harper, Tom is the rule maker; his rules, however, come from the books he has read. Thus, while Tom is fanciful in these games, he shows little original imagination and relies instead on his "book learning" for the rules governing the games. (5) Injun Joe explains to his criminal associate his evil plans to get revenge on the Widow Douglas.

Essay Questions

1. Discuss Injun Joe as the epitome of evil.

2. Discuss the methods in which Twain brings unity to the loose structure of the novel.

3. Compare the characters of Injun Joe and Muff Potter.

4. Why is Huck Finn universally admired by all of the boys in the school, but is also despised by most of the adults.

5. Why is the Widow Douglas so drawn to Huck Finn even before he was discovered to be her protector?

6. How does the Widow Douglas try to regulate Huck's life? Why does Huck want to escape?

7. What qualities does Tom Sawyer possess that make the others always choose him as the Captain, or the Chief or the General or the Number One person in any game?

8. What human qualities does Aunt Polly exhibit in her behavior toward Tom?

9. Discuss Twain's use of superstition throughout the novel and show how these superstitions affect the various actions.

10. Discuss how each of the minor characters is important to the entire novel: Judge Thatcher; Mr. Dobbins, the schoolmaster; Muff Potter; Mr. Jones, the Welshman; Amy Lawrence; and Joe Harper.

Practice Projects

The four main stories in the novel are the following: 1) Tom Sawyer and Becky Thatcher's relationship. 2) The episode on Jackson's Island and its results. 3) The Murder Plot. 4) The search and discovery of buried treasure.

1. Using these episodes, discuss Tom's development from the beginning of each episode and his maturity at the end of each episode.

2. Using the four main stories as your starting point, point out the similarities in each episode and how each is related to the others: Choose various episodes, such as "Whitewashing the Fence" or "Mr. Dobbins' Golden Dome," and show how each episode relates to one of the major episodes. Essentially what is Twain's purpose in introducing incidents which do not necessarily contribute to the main stories.

3. Assume that 10 years have passed since the final action in the novel. Describe the adults Tom and Huck would have grown into.

CliffsNotes Resource Center

The learning doesn't need to stop here. CliffsNotes Resource Center shows you the best of the best—links to the best information in print and online about the author and/or related works. And don't think that this is all we've prepared for you; we've put all kinds of pertinent information at www.cliffsnotes.com. Look for all the terrific resources at your favorite bookstore or local library and on the Internet. When you're online, make your first stop www.cliffsnotes.com where you'll find more incredibly useful information about *The Adventures of Tom Sawyer*.

Books

This CliffsNotes book provides a meaningful interpretation of *The Adventures of Tom Sawyer*. If you are looking for information about the author and/or related works, check out these other publications:

A Facsimile of the Author's Holograph Manuscript, edited by Paul Baender. Students of Mark Twain could profit by references to the original manuscript. Twain's handwriting is very legible, and its readability makes it easy to use this facsimile. Study of the text is especially important for students interested in the various stages of development and the revisions of a classic literary work. 2 vols. Washington, D.C.: Georgetown University Press, 1982.

The Adventures of Tom Sawyer, edited by John Gerber. This is the definitive edition based upon Twain's original manuscript and published along with the original illustrations by True W. Williams. From the text established by Paul Baender. Berkeley: University of California Press, 1962.

Mark Twain's America, by Bernard A. De Voto. Originally published by Little, Brown and Company in 1935, this work depicts the social and historical forces (especially the Civil War) that produced such works as *Tom Sawyer* and *Huck Finn.* This book is so completely essential to any study of Mark Twain that it was re-issued in 1997. Lincoln, NE, and London: University of Nebraska Press, 1997.

Mark Twain's (Burlesque) Autobiography, by Samuel L. Clemens. Originally published in 1871, this is Clemens' own view of his persona Mark Twain. The current edition offers an introduction by Michael J. Kiskis, which gives the reader further insight into the life of the author. Madison, WI: University of Wisconsin Press, 1990.

Mark Twain: A Literary Life, by Everett H. Emerson, is the most recent study of Twain's writing. See especially pages 90–98 which discuss Tom Sawyer in terms of his youthful innocence and his mature decisions. Contains an excellent bibliography. Philadelphia: University of Pennsylvania Press, 2000.

Mark Twain: The Development of a Writer, by Henry Nash Smith. In spite of the fact that this is an older book, Professor Smith's study is central to Twain studies. His book purports to show how Twain became a great writer and artist, and to do so he finds little or nothing positive to praise about *Tom Sawyer.* He points out that there are too many indiscretions or contradictory elements. If a student of Twain's artistry wants to find fault with *Tom Sawyer,* this book provides ample opportunities. Cambridge: Harvard University Press, 1962.

Critical Essays on The Adventures of Tom Sawyer, edited by Gary Scharnhorst. A collection of significant essays including two of the above mentioned. This is an excellent resource book. New York: G.K Hall, 1993.

Mark Twain at Work, by Bernard A. De Voto. Of particular interest in this collection of essays is the essay "The Fantasy of Boyhood: Tom Sawyer," which is an early but significant statement of the theme of the wonders of boyhood recaptured. If only one essay is to be read about Tom Sawyer, this one should be considered a must. Cambridge: Harvard University Press, 1942.

It's easy to find books published by Wiley Publishing, Inc. You'll find them in your favorite bookstores (on the Internet and at a store near you). We also have three Web sites that you can use to read about all the books we publish:

■ www.cliffsnotes.com

■ www.dummies.com

■ www.wiley.com

Internet

Check out these Web resources for more information about Mark Twain and *The Adventures of Tom Sawyer*:

About Mark Twain, www.marktwain.about.com—The most extensive site dedicated to the study of Mark Twain. Twain scholar, Jim Zwick, provides numerous links, including a history of banned books, historical contexts of the nineteenth century, Twain biographies, and timelines.

Tom Sawyer Home Page, http://etext.virginia.edu/railton/ tomsawyer/tomhompg.html—Not only does this site offer the complete text of *The Adventures of Tom Sawyer*, but it also provides information regarding its initial publishing (including its advertising and sales potential), original and contemporary reviews, selected original drawings by True Williams, and more. An interesting site for those interested not only in the text, but in its history as well.

Mark Twain: The Adventures of Tom Sawyer, www.bibliomania. com—This site offers the complete text of Tom Sawyer online, as well as a handy search feature.

Next time you're on the Internet, don't forget to drop by www.cliffs notes.com. We created an online Resource Center that you can use today, tomorrow, and beyond.

Magazines and Journals

Check out these articles for more information about Mark Twain and *The Adventures of Tom Sawyer*:

Blair, Walter. "On the Structure of Tom Sawyer." *Modern Philology*, 37 (1939): 75–88. Even though this is an early essay, it has never been superseded by later discussions of the intended structure of the novel. It is a must for any student interested in the confusing and sprawling structure of *Tom Sawyer*.

Burde, Louis J. "Slavery and the Boys: Tom Sawyer and the Germ of Huck Finn." American Literary Realism, 24 (1991): 86–90. A brief account of early uses of slavery which is first mentioned in *Tom Sawyer* and later becomes a controlling factor in *Huck Finn*.

Fertterly, Judith. "Disenchantment: Tom Sawyer in *Huck Finn. PMLA*, 87 (1972): 69–74. This article provides a view of Tom Sawyer through Huck's eyes, which presents Tom in a more realistic manner.

Gribben, Alan. "'I Did Wish Tom Sawyer Was There': Boy Elements in *Tom Sawyer* and *Huck Finn*." Found in One Hundred Years of Huck Finn: Columbia, University of Missouri Press, 1985: 149–70. This essay gives a basic and valid contrast of Tom's "book learning" with Huck's natural and common sense approach to life.

Hill, Hamlin. "Composition and Structure of Tom Sawyer." *American Literature*, 32 (1961–1962): 379–392. This article explores the relationship between the composition of certain scenes and how they are relevant to the overall structure. Compare this article with the above article by Walter Blair.

San Juan, Postora. "A Source for *Tom Sawyer*." *American Literature*, 38 (1966–1967): 101–102. This brief note is relevant for students interested in the influence of real life on certain scenes in the novel.

Send Us Your Favorite Tips

In your quest for knowledge, have you ever experienced that sublime moment when you figure out a trick that saves time or trouble? Perhaps you realized you were taking ten steps to accomplish something that could have taken two. Or you found a little-known workaround that achieved great results. If you've discovered a useful resource that gave you insight into or helped you understand *The Adventures of Tom Sawyer* and you'd like to share it, the CliffsNotes staff would love to hear from you. Go to our Web site at www.cliffsnotes.com and click the Talk to Us button. If we select your tip, we may publish it as part of CliffsNotes Daily, our exciting, free e-mail newsletter. To find out more or to subscribe to a newsletter, go to on the Web.

Index

(continued)

NOTES

NOTES

CliffsNotes

LITERATURE NOTES

Absalom, Absalom!
The Aeneid
Agamemnon
Alice in Wonderland
All the King's Men
All the Pretty Horses
All Quiet on the
  Western Front
All's Well &
  Merry Wives
American Poets of the
  20th Century
American Tragedy
Animal Farm
Anna Karenina
Anthem
Antony and Cleopatra
Aristotle's Ethics
As I Lay Dying
The Assistant
As You Like It
Atlas Shrugged
Autobiography of
  Ben Franklin
Autobiography of
  Malcolm X
The Awakening
Babbit
Bartleby & Benito
  Cereno
The Bean Trees
The Bear
The Bell Jar
Beloved
Beowulf
The Bible
Billy Budd & Typee
Black Boy
Black Like Me
Bleak House
Bless Me, Ultima
The Bluest Eye & Sula
Brave New World
Brothers Karamazov

The Call of the Wild &
  White Fang
Candide
The Canterbury Tales
Catch-22
Catcher in the Rye
The Chosen
The Color Purple
Comedy of Errors...
Connecticut Yankee
The Contender
The Count of
  Monte Cristo
Crime and Punishment
The Crucible
Cry, the Beloved
  Country
Cyrano de Bergerac
Daisy Miller &
  Turn...Screw
David Copperfield
Death of a Salesman
The Deerslayer
Diary of Anne Frank
Divine Comedy-I.
  Inferno
Divine Comedy-II.
  Purgatorio
Divine Comedy-III.
  Paradiso
Doctor Faustus
Dr. Jekyll and Mr. Hyde
Don Juan
Don Quixote
Dracula
Electra & Medea
Emerson's Essays
Emily Dickinson Poems
Emma
Ethan Frome
The Faerie Queene
Fahrenheit 451
Far from the Madding
  Crowd
A Farewell to Arms
Farewell to Manzanar
Fathers and Sons
Faulkner's Short Stories

Faust Pt. I & Pt. II
The Federalist
Flowers for Algernon
For Whom the Bell Tolls
The Fountainhead
Frankenstein
The French
  Lieutenant's Woman
The Giver
Glass Menagerie &
  Streetcar
Go Down, Moses
The Good Earth
The Grapes of Wrath
Great Expectations
The Great Gatsby
Greek Classics
Gulliver's Travels
Hamlet
The Handmaid's Tale
Hard Times
Heart of Darkness &
  Secret Sharer
Hemingway's
  Short Stories
Henry IV Part 1
Henry IV Part 2
Henry V
House Made of Dawn
The House of the
  Seven Gables
Huckleberry Finn
I Know Why the
  Caged Bird Sings
Ibsen's Plays I
Ibsen's Plays II
The Idiot
Idylls of the King
The Iliad
Incidents in the Life of
  a Slave Girl
Inherit the Wind
Invisible Man
Ivanhoe
Jane Eyre
Joseph Andrews
The Joy Luck Club
Jude the Obscure

Julius Caesar
The Jungle
Kafka's Short Stories
Keats & Shelley
The Killer Angels
King Lear
The Kitchen God's Wife
The Last of the
  Mohicans
Le Morte d'Arthur
Leaves of Grass
Les Miserables
A Lesson Before Dying
Light in August
The Light in the Forest
Lord Jim
Lord of the Flies
The Lord of the Rings
Lost Horizon
Lysistrata & Other
  Comedies
Macbeth
Madame Bovary
Main Street
The Mayor of
  Casterbridge
Measure for Measure
The Merchant
  of Venice
Middlemarch
A Midsummer Night's
  Dream
The Mill on the Floss
Moby-Dick
Moll Flanders
Mrs. Dalloway
Much Ado About
  Nothing
My Ántonia
Mythology
Narr. ...Frederick
  Douglass
Native Son
New Testament
Night
1984
Notes from the
  Underground

CliffsNotes™
@ cliffsnotes.com

The Odyssey
Oedipus Trilogy
Of Human Bondage
Of Mice and Men
The Old Man and
the Sea
Old Testament
Oliver Twist
The Once and
Future King
One Day in the Life of
Ivan Denisovich
One Flew Over
Cuckoo's Nest
100 Years of Solitude
O'Neill's Plays
Othello
Our Town
The Outsiders
The Ox Bow Incident
Paradise Lost
A Passage to India
The Pearl
The Pickwick Papers
The Picture of
Dorian Gray
Pilgrim's Progress
The Plague
Plato's Euthyphro...
Plato's The Republic
Poe's Short Stories
A Portrait of the
Artist...
The Portrait of a Lady
The Power and
the Glory
Pride and Prejudice
The Prince
The Prince and
the Pauper
A Raisin in the Sun
The Red Badge of
Courage
The Red Pony
The Return of the
Native
Richard II
Richard III

The Rise of
Silas Lapham
Robinson Crusoe
Roman Classics
Romeo and Juliet
The Scarlet Letter
A Separate Peace
Shakespeare's
Comedies
Shakespeare's Histories
Shakespeare's
Minor Plays
Shakespeare's Sonnets
Shakespeare's Tragedies
Shaw's Pygmalion &
Arms...
Silas Marner
Sir Gawain...Green
Knight
Sister Carrie
Slaughterhouse-Five
Snow Falling on Cedars
Song of Solomon
Sons and Lovers
The Sound and the Fury
Steppenwolf &
Siddhartha
The Stranger
The Sun Also Rises
T.S. Eliot's Poems &
Plays
A Tale of Two Cities
The Taming of the
Shrew
Tartuffe, Misanthrope...
The Tempest
Tender Is the Night
Tess of the D'Urbervilles
Their Eyes Were
Watching God
Things Fall Apart
The Three Musketeers
To Kill a Mockingbird
Tom Jones
Tom Sawyer
Treasure Island &
Kidnapped
The Trial

Tristram Shandy
Troilus and Cressida
Twelfth Night
Ulysses
Uncle Tom's Cabin
The Unvanquished
Utopia
Vanity Fair
Vonnegut's Works
Waiting for Godot
Walden
Walden Two
War and Peace
Who's Afraid of
Virginia...
Winesburg, Ohio
The Winter's Tale
The Woman Warrior
Worldly Philosophers
Wuthering Heights
A Yellow Raft in
Blue Water

Check Out the All-New CliffsNotes Guides

TECHNOLOGY TOPICS
Balancing Your Check-
book with Quicken
Buying and Selling
on eBay
Buying Your First PC
Creating a Winning
PowerPoint 2000
Presentation
Creating Web Pages
with HTML
Creating Your First
Web Page
Exploring the World
with Yahoo!
Getting on the Internet
Going Online with AOL
Making Windows 98
Work for You

Setting Up a
Windows 98
Home Network
Shopping Online Safely
Upgrading and
Repairing Your PC
Using Your First iMac
Using Your First PC
Writing Your First
Computer Program

PERSONAL FINANCE TOPICS
Budgeting & Saving
Your Money
Getting a Loan
Getting Out of Debt
Investing for the
First Time
Investing in
401(k) Plans
Investing in IRAs
Investing in
Mutual Funds
Investing in the
Stock Market
Managing Your Money
Planning Your
Retirement
Understanding
Health Insurance
Understanding
Life Insurance

CAREER TOPICS
Delivering a Winning
Job Interview
Finding a Job
on the Web
Getting a Job
Writing a Great Resume